MY BIZ NAVAL NATIONAL SERVICE

by

PETER CHIVERS

Cheshire Country Publishing, Chester

ISBN 0 949001 20 1

First published in the United Kingdom in 2003
by Cheshire Country Publishing

Copyright © 2003 Cheshire Country Publishing
& Peter Chivers

All rights reserved. No part of this publication may be
reproduced, stored in a retrieval system or transmitted,
in any form or by any means, without the prior permission
in writing of Cheshire Country Publishing and the Author.

A catalogue record of this book is
available from the British Library.

CONTENTS

FOREWORD   Page iii

CHAPTER ONE
SS Antilochus   Page 5

CHAPTER TWO
SS Arawa   Page 40

CHAPTER THREE
SS Villar   Page 63

CHAPTER FOUR
The Royal Navy   Page 103

Appendix   Page 132

FOREWORD

THE Second World War had only just started when I became a medical student and it was over when I qualified. My time at university was very different from that of students to-day. .

I was very conscious of my school friends who had been called up and were risking their lives. The public also sometimes made me aware of this when socialising. Part of the summer vacation was replaced by an extra term. There were Home Guard or Army Cadet duties in free time. Social life was severely curtailed because of a desire to keep a low profile.

Petrol rationing meant little private motoring. There was public transport but the "black out" made walking difficult at night time. The result of these privations was nothing, of course , compared with war service. However when the war was over National Service was continued. Like all young bachelors who had never been abroad I had a great desire to see the world. It occurred to me that this could be achieved by joining the Merchant Navy. This account is derived from the many long letters sent back to my family and kept by them for over 50 years.

PETER CHIVERS

The author, Peter Chivers.

CHAPTER ONE
SS Antilochus

SS Antilochus.

In 1947, aged 23, and having qualified as a doctor only six months before, in front of me loomed the prospect of two years in one of His Majesty's Forces.

Which one to choose?

Most of my year opted for one of the normal three Services but one other doctor and myself decided to take a chance and join the Merchant Navy. At that time it counted as National Service, which it had during the war. Both of us joined the Blue Funnel Line, at Liverpool.

My ship was called SS Antilochus. All Alfred Holt's Blue Funnel ships were named after Greek mythological figures. I was told Antilochus kept a brothel! This ship was 41 years old and had already done 87 voyages. This was to be her penultimate one. She had been built by R&W Hawthorn, Leslie & Co. Ltd. at Newcastle, with a tonnage of 9,011grt, a length of 485ft 4ins, a beam of 53ft 4ins and a service speed of 14 knots.

On September 10th, 1915 she had successfully avoided a gunfire attack by a German submarine in the Mediterranean. During the Second World War, on May 29th, 1942, she had rescued the survivors of the Mentor, another Blue Funnel ship, which had been sunk off Florida.

So on a cold February evening I walked up the gangway of this immense ship and was met on the deck by two officers. Since I was wearing a Merchant Navy uniform with two curly gold stripes and a red one in between on my sleeve it was obvious who I was. "Welcome aboard, Doc," said one. Rarely had I been called 'Doc' in hospital, but I was to hear it always in the Merchant Navy. He introduced himself as the Second Mate and his companion as the Mersey Pilot. The pilot and the mate had a problem. So much cargo had been loaded that there was only five inches of clearance on the hull of the ship due to a five-degree tilt to port.

I was shown to my cabin. Nine by five feet would be about the dimensions. In this space was a solid bunk about three feet high with drawers underneath, a desk that opened to reveal a basin the exit of which was to a bucket in the lower part. One door led on to a deck and another one to a central alleyway and these together with two portholes let in light and plenty of air. This cabin was part of the first upper deck which berthed the three mates, the chief engineer, a passenger and myself.

My cabin on the port side opened on to an open deck but on the other side of this accommodation there was a lifeboat on the deck. So I was very lucky to have my own sun lounge. Below was the saloon where we had meals and above was the Captain's quarters and above him the bridge. Forty Chinese stokers were berthed on hammocks aft and the rest of the twelve officers were in cabins further forward. The layout of the ship wasn't complicated since most of the space was cargo. There was a well deck astern of my accommodation, which housed the so-called bathroom. More of this anon! By the stern hold was my dispensary. It was in effect a long cupboard measuring six feet by three. Its proximity to the hold was an important factor later in the voyage.

Examining my bunk revealed two interesting features. Firstly that when my six foot two inches lay on the six-foot bunk my feet stuck out by the alley door. The second was the way that beds were made by Chinese servants. The sheet was not tucked into the sides of the bunk. It encompassed the blanket and both of them were laid on top of the bunk. The mattress was soft and since the weather was always warm there was little need for any extra blankets. My very silent elderly Chinese servant was always attentive and quietly efficient. Each morning he brought me a cup of tea and a metal jug of very hot water for my shave and wash. We left Liverpool early in the morning but I was able to say farewell to the wonderful Liver birds.

It wasn't a normal breakfast since the Captain was on the bridge. It took a little time to accommodate to the rapid way that the Chinese waiters attended to each course. No sooner was the knife and fork put on the plate than it was whisked away and the menu card presented for the next order. All meals were far too heavy particularly since there was no facility to enable me to burn off the excess calories.

The next duty, which was repeated every day on this voyage, was to open up the dispensary. It was barely wide enough to turn round in. Shelves both side and a few drawers held the medicines. It was rather like playing at shops! All the medicines and ointments had their labels indicating their use. So one very large Winchester was for "Coughs" and a large jar of smelly ointment was for "Piles". Obviously this ship did not always carry a doctor. My patients this morning were a few Chinese with colds. What one would expect for these sun-loving Orientals.

The pilot left us at Holyhead and we were on our own with the next stop Port Said. Much time was spent talking to any officer who had the time. The wireless operator was one of those. He was a Welshman with a good sense of humour known to all as Taffy. He told me of our passengers. The one in the next cabin to me was an accountant from Wigan who was going to a job in Singapore with a subsidiary of Alfred Holt. Normally fee-paying passengers

'Taffy', the Wireless Operator.

were discouraged on this type of ancient coal burner. One would not call it a four star hotel. We had also two pedigree spaniels called June and Bobbie. They were reputedly worth £250 each and were going out to Singapore to be trained as shooting dogs. They became the pets of the first and second mates who spoilt them rotten.

The last passenger was rather special since he took up so little space. He was a Mr Price who had been Chief Steward on this ship. His wife had died whilst as a passenger also on this ship when it was off Cape Finisterre. She had been buried at sea. Cape Finisterre had an ugly reputation in those days since one of Alfred Holt's ships had caught fire and sunk in that area only a few months before. Mr Price also died on the ship on the same voyage as the then Chief Engineer. The latter's death, according to the Second Engineer had resulted in a ghost called the "Extra Chief" which he swore he had seen in the engine room. Mr Price had wished his ashes to be strewn in the same area as his wife. His oak casket was kept on a shelf in the Captain's cabin.

The Captain with one of our passengers !

We were to have had four racehorses as passengers too but they developed 'flu and could not come. However we had a dozen kittens, which could be called passengers. They lived with the Chief Engineer and seemed to spend a lot of time in his chest of drawers.

Having had a breakfast I gave the saloon my full attention at the next meal. It appeared to be about 17 feet long and about 10 feet wide with a long table. On one side of the table were chairs on which sat the more senior officers, the Captain in the middle and me on his right. The rest of the officers sat on a long bench on the other side. The menu was in French but was not too difficult to translate and anyway the officers knew it all and one only had to point to the item to get it. The times of meals were very rigid – breakfast 8.30, lunch 12.30, supper 6 p.m. Each one had four courses, which varied over each week. Breakfast always included flapjacks and supper a fish course after the soup.

I well remember being asked by the mate "Doc, you must be a clever chap tell me, why is a mouse when it spins.?" For much of the voyage a new recruit was subjected to little pin pricks like this to establish his lack of maritime maturity. One of these was to answer silly questions. The answer I discovered later was " Because the higher the fewer!" This retort would be made with a deprecating contempt and was enough to make a rookie feel not only confused but also wondering if he had entered a madhouse.

The daily routine was "cup of tea, Docta" at 7.30, breakfast 8.30, dispensary 9.30, walk and talk until lunch at 12.30,sleep from 1.30 to 4, dispensary 4 to 4.30, read and talk until supper at 6, more talk and reading until lights out about 10. There was a radio in the saloon, which received the World Service. Taffy could provide some amusement with his short wave receiver. Rarely did the dispensary time exceed ten minutes. The rest of the allotted time was spent looking out to sea. Letters to home were a most important part of my activities since there was so much to record. The fruits of this effort are evidenced here.

One of the highlights of the day was to pay a call at either the toilet or the bathroom. The former was so small that in order to let oneself on to the seat it was advisable to hold on to the rope that hung from the back of the door. The floor was raised on slatted wood and so with the rolling of the ship there was always a sluicing of seawater to and fro under one's feet.

The bathroom however was quite a puzzle and it would have been wise to have had some instruction before embarking on a bath. In the ten foot square bathroom was a very deep bath with a board across its middle, a large metal jug, a steam boiler, a showerhead and a mirror. I thought that I would try to get water into the bath using the steam boiler. The controls of this heater were crude and somewhat dangerous since the water (dirty at first) was boiling hot and came out in a cascade. It also made menacing noises. Since the bath was so deep it was a slow job to get the right volume and the right temperature of water by mixing the boiling water with the cold.

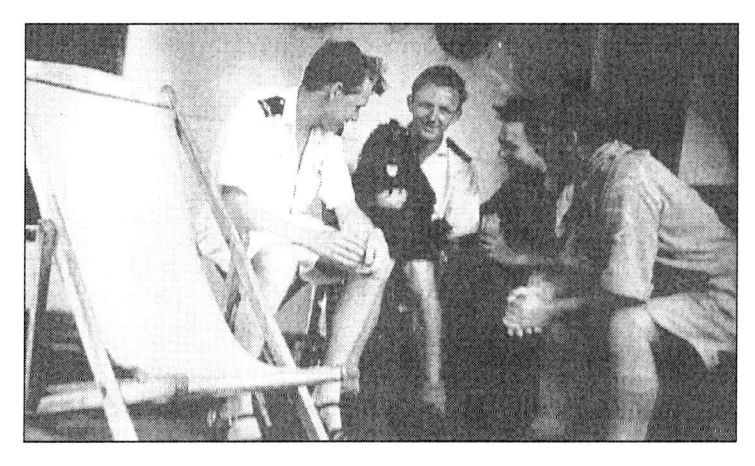

Officers with a 'passenger'.

It was not a very successful experiment made more unpleasant by the icy cold drip of water from the showerhead that was over the middle of the bath and landing on my back. A cold wind whistling under the door did not help either. Later I was informed that the correct way was to fill the jug with reasonably warm water, sit on the plank in the bath and pour the water over oneself. To operate the shower also required the use of the jug to fill the container over the showerhead. A string hanging from the ceiling operated the shower. Since fresh water was always at a premium on a coal burner it was seawater only for washing which required not only more effort to get a lather but a special soap.

The quality of the coal was an important factor in the efficient running of the engines and I was told that some of the Chinese stokers had gone off sick because they were having to work so much harder on account of the poor quality of the South Wales coal that we had taken on.

The other bit of news was that Mr Price had been dispatched to the allotted area early that morning.

Routine was disturbed when there was a weekly inspection. The Captain, Chief Officer and I went round all the ship's company's accommodation. At each place the relevant steward would accompany us and would get a telling off by the Captain if there was any dust or untidiness to be seen.

Inoculations against typhoid using a vaccine were one of my major jobs before we got to the tropics. Forty Chinese, a dozen officers and I were to be injected. Unfortunately there were side effects to this injection. It caused a slight fever, headache and soreness in the region of the injection. The latter was the main problem as far as the stokers were concerned since if the injection was into the upper arm stoking was a painful operation. If the injection was into the buttock bending and shovelling was also painful. As a result there was a minor mutiny by the Chinese and I had to forgo the injections until we were in port.

Another rather unusual job was to remove loose teeth from Chinese firemen. When they got to Hong Kong and suddenly became rich, having been paid off, the wily Chinamen spent their money on solid gold teeth As a result they would have a ready source of cash which could not be stolen – easily ! My job was to make a space for this gold. I had a pair of dental forceps and having sat the fireman on a bollard and grasping the tooth that he said needed removing I waited until the ship keeled and he went one way and I and the tooth went the other. It was all so easy and painless since the teeth were invariably loose due to gum disease.

A tour of the engine room was an exciting event. Fifty feet down vertical ladders with tubular handrails led to the working floor. The tubular handrails could be gripped by experienced engineers with an oily rag and they slid down to the bottom without feet touching the steps. On the working floor were the stokers either feeding the boilers with coal or removing red-hot ashes in wheelbarrows. The ashes would be tipped down a chute that led to the sea.

The two massive triple expansion reciprocating engines capable of producing 50,000 horsepower were in the open so that the great connecting rods could be seen going up and down. In fact one could touch the bearings and indeed the engineers would be able by so doing confirm that the cooling and lubricating oils were working efficiently. The temperature in the boiler room could get up to 130 degrees Fahrenheit when going through the Red Sea.

These engines needed steam and when we stopped in mid ocean for a couple of hours I was told that we had lost steam pressure from the boilers. In the boilers there were tubes, which if they were not fitting closely would waste steam. It was necessary to expand the tubes using a long metal tool that fitted into the end of the tube and when turned compressed its edges and sealed it. I was told later that an engineer had gone into a boiler whilst there was still some steam pressure and closed the tubes. Later I was to witness this operation and realise what temperatures were endured during the brief time that the engineer stands and performs this operation.

When this stoppage occurred the Captain was heard to mutter something about there being a Jonah on board and looking rather hard at me!

Because of the need to avoid seawater getting into accommodation there was always a 15 inch rise in the doorway. This for a tall person could cause head injury if not carefully overcome. These plus precipitous vertical narrow steps made getting about the ship, hazardous even without the added hazard of the pitching and rolling.

Little had been said to me as to where we were going and what we were carrying. We knew we were going to the Far East via the Suez Canal but since we were rather like a trader we could be sent anywhere to pick up cargo. Our present cargo of 7,000 tons, unlike that seen in modern ships had been loaded so those at the top of the hold were the goods for our first port of call. As we went on so the layers of goods were removed. The list of cargo, properly called the Manifest, seemed endless. It ranged from cars and girders through pots and pans to whisky and beer. The Chief Mate had the unenviable task of telling the stevedores at each port where goods were and making sure that they were safely delivered ashore.

This was to be the first time that I had been outside Europe and been exposed to the pressures of native vendors. In my naivety I had been influenced by the hardened officers who had said that my information was wrong about the buying of goods in the East. I felt that it was all barter and that it was very cut throat. They with very straight faces had said that the Gyp (as all North Africans were called) would state a price and that was it. This was part of the initiation of the rookie since my preconceptions were quite correct and indeed led to interesting experiences in bartering.

The first evidence of arriving at Port Said was the sight of a small boat with a number of officials on board. It seemed to me that they were involved in an argument with gesticulating hands and loud voices. I learned that this behaviour was normal. One of this group was the pilot and another the doctor. My great moment had come! I had to sign the end of a lengthy document that I was told was a medical practique. This indicated that a doctor had examined all the crew and passengers and verified that none of them had any infectious disease.

All but the pilot then departed and we approached the waterfront. We steamed slowly down a long string of buoys that led to a concrete breakwater and passed a few sunken vessels with only their funnels showing. These were the only evidence of war damage we saw. The sun was just rising and the pleasing sight was of a long strand of sand with many bathing huts and palms on it.

'Bum boats' at Port Said.

The town itself was a mass of flat-topped lightly hued houses, mainly yellow. Before we anchored we were surrounded by native dhows, which were a beautiful sight with their high sails in profile the shape of a shark's fin. Our anchorage was to one side of the main channel into the Suez Canal and right opposite us dominating centre stage was a store with SIMON ARTZ prominently displayed on its front. This was the only properly built shop in Port Said, which meant that the rest were street traders. Here was the opportunity for experience! Surrounding us as soon as we had stopped were a crowd of what I was told were "Bum boats". This expression denoted any small craft that brought itinerant traders on to the ship. Since these were not all scrupulously honest it was always advisable to not only lock one's cabin door but also securely shut the porthole.

In no time at all they had each found a spot on the deck to display their wares. These were mainly camel leather goods such as bags, purses or wallets. However there were some who had watches and jewellery. Fakes and Rolex watches for £5 were quite common!

Not having succumbed to entering into a negotiation with one of these traders I went down for breakfast and decided to go ashore with our passenger (Mr Lyon), the Purser and the Captain. The Purser had changed four of my English pounds for four Egyptian ones. I gained one shilling and six pence on the deal! I felt that with these knowledgeable experienced travellers I would not be led astray. We were taken ashore in an Alfred Holt launch. The two officers went off on their own and left Mr Lyon and I to fend for ourselves.

The heat was the first impression on going ashore. On the ship because of the breeze we had still been wearing long trousers and I was wearing a suit. This was quite intolerable and soon was clinging to my body. Immediately we were besieged by a horde of youngsters who exhorted us to buy pornographic postcards or "meet" their sister. Since I had been warned about this pressure group I ignored them completely and just went on walking. Mr Lyon however decided to tell them to go away. This had no effect so he started to walk a little faster. This resulted in the lads following him and leaving me alone. The dress of these youngsters, indeed of all the Gyps we saw, was the "tarboosh" – a long white night dress like garment that being loose was cooling by virtue of the cushion of air inside.

A Merchant Navy story was that by wearing such a garment the Saviour when he came down to earth would be entrapped in this bell like gown. To hear the way that negotiations went on, as one walked along was a revelation. The price for the infamous postcards would reduce at a set rate per ten yards until the limit of sixpence was reached. Usually one was addressed as Mister Captain.

The shopkeepers were as bad. Always there was a chair outside their stall on which sat the owner. On seeing us twenty yards away he would start walking towards us proclaiming his wares and their cheapness. "Captain come inside and have a shufti" A shufti was a look and was tantamount to a sale. The exhortations would go on for about another ten yards beyond the shop whereupon the shopkeeper would return to his chair. The range of goods was wide and like those of the traders on the ship many were fakes. In those days Omega watches were much desired in the UK but these Omegas, though they had the name on the face, were fakes. At Simon Artz however one could depend on the Omega watch being genuine and at £50 was worth having.

Parker 51 pens too were just coming out of America and were available in this store. In the end I bought a camel leather holdall from a native's shop after quite a long bargaining session. It cost me 175 piastas (a piasta was equivalent to 2 shillings) but the original price had been 236 piastas, which was over £5. So the bag cost me £1 ten shillings. The bag was lined, had two side pockets and a zip. However the stitching was poor and when I got it home I had to have it restitched.

Back on board there was plenty of activity. The hatches were open and the cargo of sugar was being unloaded. This ship was unusual in having what were called "goal post masts". These allowed for the use of two steam driven winches either side of the ship to be used to lift the cargo out of the ship and deposit it into a lighter lying alongside on

Discharging cargo in Port Said.

either side. The further winch from the lighter lifted the sling up to about ten feet above the deck. The other winch which was alongside the lighter had a hawser round the slings and by pulling on it was able to place it above the lighter and allow the first winch to lower it.

The winch men were very proficient but short tempered. When I wanted to walk aft to my dispensary past the open hatches I was shouted at since I was slowing down the operation. Bedlam was the only description of the scene. Vigilance to avoid pilfering and the lifting of the right cargo for that port was the Chief Mate's duty. Now one could realise how important it was to get the cargo stowed in the right sequence in Liverpool. The dangers too must not be ignored. Sheet plates came out of the sling and fell 45feet into the hold where the dockers were loading. Luckily no one was hurt but no doubt if one of those sheets had hit a man it would have killed him. Quite apart from the danger there was the waste of damaged cargo, which would have to be replaced on the next voyage. The cargo workers got 3 shillings a day pay. They never seemed to stop working.

On deck, discharging cargo.

That evening I was taken ashore with some engineers and mates. After a few beers in various bars we gravitated to what seemed the only cabaret called "Fanfare". To say the floorshow was puerile would be complimenting it. We were all glad to get back to the ship to some quiet and sense.

Some of the men had been drinking too much and either as a result of falling or getting into a fight a couple of them were the worse for wear with facial cuts and bruises. As a result it was a good excuse for me to take them up to the local hospital for some stitching and professional dressings. The Egyptian doctor was not only efficient but also anxious to show me round. Unfort-unately there was no time but the cleanliness and efficiency was quite remarkable for such a small hospital.

View of the ship's accommodation.

The following day we coaled. This was quite a skilful but highly dangerous operation. Two barges full of coal were brought on either side of the ship's coalbunker. Planks were lashed to the side of the ship so that there were two levels before reaching the ship's deck. Six Gyps in the coal barge loaded baskets with coal that were then carried on the backs of a team. The latter carried their baskets up to the edge of the coalbunker and tipped them in. They threw their empty basket into the coal barge and hopped down in great strides back into the coal barge. This was done at speed and inevitably since it went on all day one of the carriers would fall into the coal hold or the bunker. Luckily this happened when I was watching but with no apparent effect except to cause much merriment. All the time the team chanted in a way that reminded me of a record running down when the gramophone had not been wound fully.

The whole ship was covered in coal dust and it was always at this juncture in a voyage that the Captain gave the order that khaki be worn. Until then we had been wearing either mufti or whites. Sailors, rather like housewives, have a thing about cleanliness. So for some days after coaling the Chief Mate was getting the hoses on to the decks and the cleaners on to all the brass work.

We then started to enter the canal. In front of us was HMS Theseus, a large aircraft carrier. Our speed was reduced to about seven knots so that we would not damage the walls of the canal. As we went along we saw gangs working on repairing the walls that had been damaged during the war as a result of ships going too fast. Other evidence of the war was old army camps and bombed ships with just their funnels protruding. Despite this slow speed it felt that we were going quite fast. This was because we were no more than thirty yards from either bank.

Our sister ship, Glaucus, was passed waiting for the boiler tubes that we had brought for her engine repair. The land either side was so flat that the curvature of the earth could be seen. To make us realise where we were we saw an Egyptian on a dromedary and a group of Muslims praying in the direction of (what we assumed was) Mecca. At intervals along the canal were look out towers, which presumably kept an eye on the traffic to make sure there were no hold ups.

The small town of Ishmalia was seen and its two bitter lakes. Why they were called bitter was not known but it would probably refer to the state of the water. Close by was a fifty foot high monument to those who died in the Canal Zone during the Second World War. It was impressive not only because of its height but that it was split vertically. Our first port of call after Port Said was Port Tufiq, before we got there the captain ordered a yellow flag be flown. This was commonly known as the "Yellow Duster" and was an indication that there was a doctor on board and that there was no infectious disease. So once again I appended my signature to the bottom of the long document and we were able to anchor.

It was winter in the Red Sea, which we were about to enter and therefore the temperature was only ninety Fahrenheit! In the Red Sea with a following wind the temperature near the boilers could reach 130! This weather was very conducive for sleeping and despite the best intentions to read this had been the way of life every afternoon and late evening. At the southern end of the Red Sea were a dozen rocks in the middle called the Twelve Apostles. They were also known as the Gateway to Hell and when the waves were dashing over them it was quite understandable, When we got near Aden the waves were sufficient to cover the decks and I got soaked more than once but dried almost instantly. Aden rather reminded me of Gibraltar since it had high mountains around it.

The cargo taken on in Aden was onions, potatoes and dried fish.

Coaling at Port Said.

The author...in khaki.

The latter were stacked on the fore deck just a yard in front of the saloon. We gradually got accustomed to the stench. For the second time we loaded with coal. This time there were a series of landings alongside the ship's side joined by planks. At each stage was a coolie who received a bag of coal and passed it on to his next higher mate. The dirge was more melodious than before. This coal had come from South Africa and was unwashed and therefore even dustier than that which we had in Port Said. It got everywhere and penetrated under the doorsills.

Due to having so little money left after the ravages of Port Said I went ashore with only a few rupees. However this was enough for me to see a film at the NAAFI open-air cinema. The screen was so large that we had noticed it as we arrived at the port. The film was "The Thin Man Comes Home" and featured William Powell and Myrna Loy. Wandering around this small town I felt more comfortable than at Port Said for at least two reasons. Firstly there were remarkably few touts and annoying followers, and secondly there was some comfort in the sight of the Union Jack flying over some of the buildings to indicate that this was a British colony.

Aden had a reputation for cheap goods and this was quite evident in the shops. A so called gold plated Ronson cigarette lighter cost £1 fifteen shillings, white silk shirts eighteen shillings and tennis shoes seven shillings and six pence.

Our stay in Aden was only two days and then we had the wide Indian Ocean to cross before getting to Colombo. After two days the island of Sokotra was seen and I was told that the Merchant Navy charts note that it was unfriendly. Apparently this was due to the fact that the natives became hungry and ate the lighthouse keeper. From then on the occasional steamer relieved the boredom of the wide-open sea. However shoals of flying fish made a spectacular sight when they flew in their hundreds to escape from some predator. They skimmed over the crest of the waves and occasionally in bad weather we saw them on the deck. I was told that they made good eating.

A shark or whale was the cause for some excitement but otherwise only the Roaring Forties was of interest. The waves were at least forty feet high and were so widely apart that when one was in the valley one couldn't see the horizon. Being a big ship it rode the waves well but for a smaller craft there might have been some danger.

A couple of the Chinese developed "Gyppo tummy" – a mild sort of dysentery, which quickly responded to the appropriate medicine in the dispensary. Reading and writing long letters to home occupied much of my time. Trevelyan's History of England with its 700 pages had been brought on board to balance my books on Tropical Medicine and Surgery.

So we reached Colombo in Ceylon – the "tear drop" under India's nose! As usual we were stuck out in the middle of the harbour and were soon surrounded by bumboats. The port doctor was helpful and gave me an invitation to Colombo General Hospital and instructions how to get there. Soon I learned that the Indian rupee was worth one shilling and six pence and that there were 100 cents to the rupee. To go ashore would cost 1 rupee by bumboat. A taxi to the town centre would cost 2 rupees, a beer 2 rupees 50 cents, and a seat in the cinema 2 rupees. I then calculated that my night out would cost me £1. This was indeed the form and it was an opportunity to get a feel for the town. Again like Aden it was so British that one felt quite comfortable. Not only was the speech British but the manners and even the commodities were British. The second engineer and I saw "The Cockeyed Miracle" a B class movie that no one had ever heard of.

The weather was hot and sticky with occasional showers of rain. Despite the weather the Indian stevedores wore long sarongs, which reached to their ankles. However when they were working on the ship they hitched the sarong up and tucked it into the waist to made a pair of shorts. Perhaps this was the origin of the expression "girding up

Aden.

one's loins". The Indian male that came on to the ship usually had curly oily black hair and often a handlebar moustache. Invariably he would be chewing a betel nut and this would make his white teeth show up in this red mouth. Betel juice had been associated with cancer of the mouth and one could understand why since it was so commonly used.

Shortage of lighters delayed us half a day in loading the cargo of tea for Penang. One of the many natives that always came on board at every port was the "dhobie" man. He was always welcome since he took away dirty clothes and within a day returns them in spotless condition and well pressed. Normally they were reasonable but like all traders there was always some bartering before giving an order. On this occasion I did not avail myself of the facility. The reason was that I did my own washing and ironing. In the Merchant Navy as indeed in the Royal Navy there was a "make-do and mend" afternoon when it was usual to do one's dhobieing and putting on the odd button or repair of a tear. Sailors make very good husbands for this reason !

Also on board was a rather unusual trader. Colombo had a reputation for being the centre for semi precious stones. This man was a jeweller and showed a selection of gems that looked wonderful. It would have been most useful to have had an expert with us since no one could value these attractive stones. Opals, zircons (a type of diamond) and sapphires were recognised.

A trip ashore in the agent's launch saved me a rupee and I was able to see what the town was like in daylight. The shops (no windows of course) seem to display black wooded carved elephants predominantly. Occasionally there would be a fruit stall with mangoes and bananas.

Jewellery too was quite prominent. There were some stores rather like Simon Artz at Port Said. The one that I went into was called Gargills and had a similar range of British goods. I bought the only commodity that I knew my family at home would connect with, Ceylon – tea. So I bought eight pounds of Broken Orange Pekoe that was reckoned to be the best tea in Ceylon. Two of those pounds were dispatched home and the rest I kept for gifts and myself.

This was my opportunity to visit the hospital and via a taxi I made my way to the Medical Superintendent's office. Through him I was introduced to one of the resident surgeons. He was in the middle of a list of 21 patients. He had a colleague who operated on another patient in the same rather small operating theatre. I was told that there were 2000 patients in the hospital of which 500 were accommodated in the open air. I stayed for half an hour to watch him perform a few operations and then took a tram back to the quay. I was charged 10 cents for the experience of the tram ride that must have caused quite a few bruised toes since I was wearing shoes and most of the other standing crowded passengers were barefoot. As we were so crowded I got off when we had to let someone get on. When I did this there was a shout from the passengers and luckily I realised this was directed at me since as I quickly got back on, a tram went past in the other direction missing me by inches.

It was lunchtime and I was anxious to try a proper Indian curry. This was an experience I will never forget since my knowledge of curries had been of the ship's Chinese chef's relatively mild ones. The one I had in this Indian restaurant nearly took the roof off my mouth and copious drafts of orange squash did little to assuage the heat in my

Port Swettenham.

A 'trishaw' in Colombo.

mouth, which I compared with Dante's Inferno. I learned later that bananas were the right antidote to hot curries. The fish that went with the curry reminded me too much of that we had on the hatch cover for my liking!

Just to finish the evening off I went to the Merchant Navy Club for another orange squash and to see what sort of officers frequent such places. I was neither inspired by the rather bleak interior or by the company none of whom I knew.

The nightlife of Colombo, like many other ports, was usually a trip to the cinema. The second house started at 9.30 p.m. and so I had an opportunity to visit the native quarter. One of the most memorable impressions I felt in every town I went to on this voyage, and one that was immediate, was the smell, though not unpleasant it was compounded mostly of cooked food and perhaps of spices. Unlike home all the shops were open with the wares descending from the back of the shop on to the middle of the pavement. In Colombo the most obvious items on display were black carved elephants of various sizes. I was told that though the traders always said that they were made of teak this was very rarely the case.

Fruit stalls were colourful with mangoes and bananas amongst the pineapples. In the native quarter there was a celebration, which I was told, related to the return of relics of the Brahmin god. Bunting was everywhere and there was quite a carnival atmosphere. Indian music drew us into a large barn. This was called a theatre but all the audience stood. On the stage three Indian girls with colourful costumes and many bangles on their arms performed a sinuous dance. It seemed to go on forever. I was told that this was a Devil Dance but you could have fooled me! When we got to the cinema we tried to relate it to our experience of "flea pits" at cinemas at home. One came to mind near the Preston Royal Infirmary which was so close that we doctors could be called out from there. We called it the Flea Pit and we thought that no cinema could be more run down than that. How wrong I was! This was dilapidated and, of course, the film was a B movie that no one had ever heard of featuring "Our Gang".

Quite an evening of down market entertainment but for the native it was, no doubt, a great treat. Perhaps the high light of the evening was the journey back to the quay in a rickshaw. Two features of the old rickshaw will always appeal. Firstly the quiet, only the padding of the Indian's feet disturbed the silence. The other was the panoramic view one got from this pleasantly high seat, but cycles were beginning to take the place of the man drawn rickshaw.

Alongside the road were seen parts of aeroplanes, boats and bridges. These were being assembled in preparation for an invasion of Malaya, which, of course, did not take place.

As we left Colombo the following day we were made aware of our ship's shabby appearance by the sight of the cruiser HMS Jamaica ahead of us. She was immaculate with sparkling grey paint that even was seen on the chains of the anchors.

We picked up two passengers at Colombo. One a scientist and the other an engineer and what a difference they made to the trip to Penang. After six weeks at sea I was noticing that, like my fellow officers I was beginning to become introverted and taciturn. Sometimes a meal would go by with no one speaking other than to make some relevant remark about the food.

It was difficult to imagine unless one had been in an institution or on a protracted expedition or even in prison what it was like to be confined in a relatively small space (and an uncongenial small space) with men who know each other very well and doing work that was monotonous. All the officers on the ship had talked through all aspects of their domestic lives and their attitudes to politics, religion and marriage. Only when mail came from home was there something to talk about and that usually was news that we might have heard on the radio. Inevitably home politics, particularly an impending election would spark off some discussion. It was quite obvious to me that as a new boy I had to provide some interesting conversation. Much was made of educating the Doc in the ways of the East and usually contradicting my naïve preconceptions. So the advent of two passengers took me off the hook and much time was spent hearing the experiences of these two men.

It seemed to me that in middle age there was a stereotype of Englishman in the Orient. He tended to be tallish and about 17 stone in weight. These two were of this build. The scientist was attached to a rubber plantation. Despite his large size now he told me that in Changi gaol in Singapore where he was after being captured by the Japanese he went down to 9 stones. The engineer was attached to one of Alfred Holt's subsidiaries in Penang. He gave me a book called "The Egg and I" by Mary Macdonald. It was the story of a hen farmer in the Olympic peninsula, which was off Puget Sound in North West America. Later in my travels I would see the lovely mountains on the Olympic peninsula from Victoria on Vancouver Island.

An island was identified as Sumatra and we were advised that despite the end of the Japanese war, there were still Japanese there who would take a pot shot at any Allied ship that went close inshore!

One of the wonders of the Orient was the sunset. Although only lasting minutes the sun going down below the horizon produced an artist's palette of colours.

The next day we arrived at Georgetown, which was the port of Penang. It was quite remarkable for a number of reasons. High mountains each of which had a puff of cumulus cloud on its summit surrounded it. Though there were sandy beaches there appeared to be jungle close by the edge of the town. Because the only two berths alongside the jetty were occupied we had to stay out in the straits about half a mile from the shore. Luckily the agent's launch with our mail brought back our good spirits. On it was our mail from home. It was difficult to overemphasise the importance of this link with home. It was looked upon rather in the same way as exam results. They were seized upon and read avidly not once but many times savouring the important bits. Partly the reason for this thirst for news from home was that only the chief wireless operator and the chief mate had access to a radio and it was very difficult to phase a visit to either of them to coincide with them having the radio on and it to be transmitting news.

Penang had a particular interest for me since I had a favourite uncle who had been the manager for the Automobile Association (AA) there before the war. He had been captured by the Japanese and had had an unpleasant time working on the Burmese/Siam railway. His wife and three children managed to get to Australia and eventually back to the UK. He too after the war went back there and started up a holiday camp business. Before I left home he had given me names of some of his colleagues whom he thought might have returned to Penang.

So armed with this list I went ashore using a sampan. I had been told that there was only one really good hotel in Penang, namely the E&O (the Eastern & Oriental) and so it was to that splendid establishment I went. It was everything that I felt was the opulence of the East. It was cool as a result of marble floors and wide-open doorways leading to shady covered areas. To assist the movement of the air were punkahs. These were long strips of heavy material suspended from the ceiling and capable of being moved sideways by ropes and pulleys operated by punkah wallahs. The two punkah wallahs in the large lounge were seated opposite each other on either side of the room and pulled the ropes so that the material waved in rhythmic slow fashion.

Here I met two of my uncle's old colleagues. It was all so different from the surroundings on board ship that I had to keep pinching myself. Naturally the conversation was nostalgic but they were able to give me some information that I could convey back to my uncle. It seemed that the lack of cars resulting from the war had severely reduced the AA's business. A swim in the hotel's pool, the first swim since leaving home, was disappointing in the warmth of the water. At 70 degrees there was little feeling of exhilaration. I was taken to the International Club where I was given to understand all the ex pats were to be found. A Carlsberg beer made me realise that there was still a great deal of Dutch influence here. Finally I was taken back to the E and O where a dance was to be held. This event made me feel very much the outsider since all the parties were in couples and I got the impression that the women were very spoilt and, unlike home, were somewhat aloof.

I was able to have one dance however - and then retired to bed. Once again a first time since leaving home a proper comfortable bed with proper sheets and plenty of room for my legs. The shock came in the morning when I got the bill. 16 dollars in those days was a great deal of money. In many ways it was worth it to have a large bedroom with a veranda and to luxuriate under a shower that was both the right temperature and pressure and went on indefinitely.

When I got back to the ship the cargo of tea, girders and paint were being unloaded. When that was completed we set sail for Port Swetenham that was only a few miles down the coast. The name Swetenham was apt and faithful to its climate. I thought that Penang was hot but Port Swetenham was far worse. Perhaps the only thing that could be said in its favour was that for the first time we were able to go alongside the jetty. It meant, of course, that we were able to go ashore at any time. Oddly enough I made little use of this facility. Reasons for this were the heat, the humidity, the mosquitoes, the torrential rain and lastly there was nothing to see ashore! The mosquitoes were vicious and very soon my supply of insect repellent was depleted. Despite this the chief mate had to be treated for a very swollen eye and mouth. I had 13 bites on the first day. Lying on my bunk with the doors and porthole open and the fan on was the only way to keep cool.

The second engineer had banged his elbow and I told him he must not do heavy work with that arm. He said that the five-inch nut on the big end of one of the engine's connecting rods had to be tightened. It needed a six-foot spanner that had to be hit with a 28-pound sledgehammer to move it. I told him that as I was short of exercise I would do it for him. In the engine room with the fires still lit the temperature was very very hot. The Chinese stokers were standing by but were considered too weak for this type of job. I was wearing rubber lacrosse shoes (we played lacrosse at my school) and the floor was oily. The result was that I hit the spanner but went sprawling on the floor. Great loss of face! It was ignominious but inevitable that the Chinese stokers did the job, albeit slowly and grudgingly!

The houses in the village were all new and had been erected by the Japanese. The true atmosphere of the place could only be obtained in the so-called shopping area in the centre. Here on either side of the street was a wide gully about three feet deep and two feet wide, which accepted the drains of the houses and the copious rainfall. This was a favourite place for a drunken sailor to fall into and break an ankle. Fruit stalls were the main attraction and for four shillings and six pence (two dollars) I got a three-foot high stalk containing at least 100 bananas!

In Colombo I had been in a conventional rickshaw with a man pulling. Here the Japanese had introduced the trishaw, a three wheeled appliance, much more efficient but far less traditional Old cows and bullocks, so under fed that they looked like St Bernard dogs, walked the streets together with goats and scurvy hounds. The latter with clumps of flies on their backs cringed before the oncoming pedestrians.

The shops were unusual since there was not one that stuck to one commodity despite my first impressions. For example the hairdresser though he had three chairs for his customers on one side of the shop also had on the other cycles in various states of repair. Haberdashery and fruit seemed to be a popular combination. The combination of the fruit and animal smells together with that of humans was something special to the Orient. With rubber being the principal product in this part of the world it was not surprising that rubber shoes (actually open toed sandals) were not only popular but also cheap. I bought a pair for 2 dollars and noted that they were made in a place called Klang, 5 miles from there. Many of the goods had been imported from Hong Kong.

The second and third mates with whom I was shopping stopped me outside a shop that was completely covered in bottles. Besides the local brew (Saki) there was every sort of liquor and brandy. One may bring in through the customs any size of bottle provided it had been opened and a drink taken from it. A small bottle of Benedictine liquor only cost 8 dollars (£1) Whilst there we sampled the Tiger beer – the local brew – which was very expensive at 1.40 dollars a glass. The general feeling was that we would wait until we got to Hong Kong before buying any Duty Free drink.

Bird and animal life on the mud bank by the ship was fascinating, Small reptiles about four inches long moved about using what seemed to be fins. Crabs with very long claws scuttled about and hawks came down like dive-bombers. When the galley boy was bringing a tray of food to the saloon one of these hawks swooped down and took away some food. Chameleons were seen on walls where they catch flies. Plants too had been intriguing; a hedge of a sensitive plant would collapse if one brushed against it. After a few minutes it would gradually come back to its erect state.

The stevedores were Indian, Chinese, Indonesian and occasionally Japanese but rarely Malay. The Japanese were the toughest and best workers and the Malays were the ones that tried to get the lightest work - i.e. tally clerking. In the hold away from the eagle eye of the mate the stevedores stole cigarettes. They use their strong grappling hooks to prize open the top of a packing case. If the mate sees the theft one was favoured with a burst of very loud invective that would be the envy of a sergeant major in the army. There might well be a fine to go with the telling off.

All Indians were called George and the Chinese, Tommy. Every sentence, which had to be bellowed would end with the words "eh, eh,

Tommy/George." What surprised me was how the fourth mate not yet 21 was able to cow a group of Indians using this invective. It would be interesting to try it out at home on an inefficient waiter!

We were now passing through the Straits of Mulacca and would be in Singapore at 6 a.m. I was told that we should be there for about three weeks. On the last voyage they had to wait outside the port for a month because there was a stevedores' strike. Wheedling our way through the islands of the archipelago of the Dutch East Indies we found ourselves in the quarantine area surrounded by ships. The port doctor took about an hour to reach us – about par for the course in my short experience. Shortly after this the agent came aboard. At each port Alfred Holt had an agent who administered to the ship whilst it was in the port. He dealt with cargo details and all aspects of replenishing of stores or coal. He also brought the mail – his most important function. This time he told us that we would go alongside the jetty at 6 p.m. and would start unloading cargo at 7. The first impression of Singapore sea front was of a few large buildings with a number of lightly coloured smaller buildings around. In the event these large buildings were the Cathay Theatre, Law Courts, Adelphi Hotel and the Cathedral. Sure enough at 6 p.m. we went alongside accompanied by a P & O boat – the Otranto.

That evening was spent on the dock trying to get in touch with friends of my uncle. The following morning dressed in my whites I went ashore with the Captain. Torrential rain came down non-stop until 3 p.m. We went to the Alfred Holt office and there I met a Walter Chivers. This was quite unexpected and though he was not a relative of mine despite the fact that he looked rather like my paternal grandfather we got on very well. He invited me to his flat where I met his wife. They had both been interned in Malaysia during the war and she had had typhus.

Their flat was right on the front next to the Adelphi Hotel and therefore had a magnificent panoramic view of the harbour. I was taken by them to the Singapore swimming pool and there met a number of their friends and since the Chivers were in their sixties I was not fortunate enough to meet any young people. An amusing incident occurred when I was there. I had let the doorman know that I was a doctor from the Antilochus in case I was wanted for any medical reason. It was therefore quite a surprise to see a man walking around the pool with a board on which was written Doctor Chivers! I went to the manager's office expecting that I would be summoned back to the ship but no. Apparently one of the staff had walked on a piece of glass and had cut her foot badly. The manager had panicked and first of all put a tourniquet round her leg and then remembering that I was on site called me. In the event it was nothing like as serious as he had made out and responded to a little pressure and leg raising. As I was a guest I felt I could not charge for this professional service.

The shops in Singapore were like going into Aladdin's cave. They seemed to have everything possible for sale except eggs and butter. I was told that the reason for this was due to a strike in the docks at Sydney, Australia. The shops tended to be grouped according to the commodity for sale.

Food would be followed by ironmongery and perhaps furniture. Families would be living their lives around the shops and so the scene seemed chaotic. From the upper floors of the shops bamboo poles with long strips of material had Chinese characters printed on them – vertically. The impression was rather like a carnival. Watches at home had not yet been made in quantity and to see the vast selection of American watches was a real treat. I wanted a watch with a centre second hand and indeed I found and bought one for £6 10 shillings. It was a Pierce and was gold plated.

At a food shop I sent a parcel home containing tins of bacon, cheese, jam, peaches and pears, Del Monte was the magic name on the fruit cans. These were all bought from a big shop called" Little and Co" and by good fortune I had met the owner's wife at the swimming pool! At the shoe stall I bought a pair of suede shoes that were called "brothel creepers" at that time. They had a thick rubber sole and were exceptionally comfortable and cost $16 (£2).

Thanks to the friend of the agent called Tan Aik Joo the Captain and I were invited to a Chinese lunch. Tan Aik Joo had three wives and thirteen children! This was the most memorable meal not only of the

Singapore from the ship.

Swimming pool in Singapore.

voyage but also of my life. This was held in a village called Bedok and the table was laid on the first floor. The women prepared it on the ground floor. The Captain, the agent and I were the guests and after each of the fourteen courses we had to respond to the toast "Yam Seng" which means "Good Health" in Chinese by downing our glass of whisky. The result was inevitable. This plus the insistence that we used chopsticks to pick up the food from the centre of the circular table and dip the morsel into one of the many concentric dishes of sauce on the way back to the plate; The ten Chinese other guests only sipped their whisky and so stayed relatively sober.

The courses were – shark fin soup, roast goose, stuffed chicken, steamed prawns and cauliflower, mushrooms and other vegetables

Tan Aik Joos' house in Singapore.

Mr Tans' thirteen children.

steamed with meat, stuffed duck, crab and pork, chicken pie, roast Ikankrapoh fish (a new one to me!) yam and melon, mushrooms and cabbage, stuffed meat and eggs, sweat pumpkin and chicken and finally pears. All the dishes were placed in the centre of the table and though there were a large number one ate only a very little of each because of the difficulty of using chopsticks. The state of the tablecloth could be imagined.

A highlight was a visit with the agent to the Taw Par Villa. This was a large garden with many temples. A wealthy Chinese who had invented "Tiger Balm" and as a result had become a millionaire had

Singapore 'flea market'.

built this Villa. This balm is what we would call a rubaficient nowadays. In other words it produced a very warm feeling and was effective when bruises or strains needed treating. His "Gods" had told him that he must spend his money on making pleasure places and as a result he had produced similar villas in other big towns in this part of the world. If he did this he would never die! That is what he was told!

A group of officers and myself went to an entertainment centre called the Great World. Here was a cinema, restaurant, dance hall and many small shops. In the dance hall for a dollar one could have three dances with a Chinese girl (far too small!) or an Eurasian (very few available).

After a couple of dollars worth of this we all went to a midnight movie at the cinema. Here we saw "Two Years Before the Mast". Unfortunately I had seen it before. We learned that the Chinese owner of the cinema also owned the restaurant, dance floor and a block of flats and had come to Singapore as a rickshaw coolie.

On the journey from the ship to the centre of the town- a matter of two miles and costing two dollars in a taxi we saw Chinese temples with tapestries and Indian temples with their sacred cows and many junks on the river. On them families lived in a most untidy state. The one aspect of life that could not be conveyed in words was the smell that though pungent was not objectionable. Since so much of life was conducted in the open much of that smell came from cooking and foods.

Taw Par Villa.

At Taw Par Villa with the Alfred Holt agent.

We took on a male passenger in Singapore who was interesting in so far as he had a strong antipathy to women. It appeared that he had developed his aversion in America. Details were not revealed but since he was so well read and cultured he was a good companion. His New Zealand accent and the way that he cynically said "lurve" were well remembered.

Five days later we entered Hong Kong harbour under the towering peaks and shore port West of Kowloon. We tied up at Kowloon where Alfred Holt had its own wharf. The efficiency of this wharf, which was run by private enterprise, was in strong contrast to the one at Singapore.

In a very short time I was ashore and gazing goggle-eyed at the shops. Everything that was either rationed or unobtainable at home was there. Watches of every sort, silk and nylon stockings, and tinned fruit were the first things that hit my eye. Since we once had a Chow dog at home I always had it in my mind that this sort of dog was eaten in China. In fact I thought that the word "chow" was related to this type of food but I now discovered that it meant any sort of food. My favourite was curry and prawns and for 3 dollars (3 shillings and nine pence) I could buy an 18-inch oval plate heaped high with this delicious dish. To get to Hong Kong required a 40-cent ferry ride and this was what I took with some of the mates to see "Sailors Ahoy" – a weak American film.

Although Kowloon had given me some idea of the luxuries in the shops going to Hong Kong was like going to a different world. Perhaps it was the merchants selling every imaginable commodity that was so intriguing. In the street was a stall where every part of a chicken was displayed from the feathers to the intestines – all for sale. There were many large American cars.

Parker 51 pens were all the rage and to have one with a rolled gold barrel was the tops. Also watches with a centre second hand. I bought both of these for myself and still have them. The watch an American Pierce cost the equivalent of £7.

I was struck by the enormous number of craft in the harbour in Hong Kong. There were junks, sampans, American destroyers, submarines, ferries and motorboats. The junks and sampans were of special interest as families of Chinese were born, raised and died within the confines of these craft. The sampans were about 10 ft long and were sculled along by a woman (almost invariably), standing at the stern. Another one often used one oar to help. The lightness of the sampans enabled the woman to move people at a good three knots. All the meals were prepared, ablutions performed, and other requisites of a Chinese life were encompassed in the 10 feet.

Fishing was the industry of the 1000s of sampans hence the staple diet, rice and fish. These women were scrupulously clean and their hair was their crowning glory. It literally shone with a light ebony colour. Hours were spent by these women, in the sampan by the ship just waiting for the dunnage, which would have been thrown from the ship's holds. We often made them have races from stern to stern for an empty tin can – a precious possession.

Junks were very different. They resembled galleons of the Spanish Armada on a small scale. Most of them were capable of braving the China Seas and because of the risk of pirates were often armed with small canons. Square lantern sails and the usual sculling and rowing served to propel these larger boats. Most of the larger ones took cargo up and down the coast. Coming out of Hong Kong that day I could see well over 50 junks on the horizon.

Ships of every nationality and size were around us while at anchor. Scandinavian ships were the cleanest and were very beautiful. However they did not compare with the Dutch. Our ship looked like a dirty old carthorse at the Grand National!

The vista was not appreciated from the ship as only the mountains of China and Hong Kong surround the Channel. When I climbed the Peak via the funicular railway all the range of mountains in China and the many small islands around Hong Kong could be seen. The railway goes up to within a few hundred feet of the summit and during the 10 minutes it took to ascend the last 1,000 feet it was at an angle of over 45 degrees. The problem of the cable breaking was, of course, raised! The mountains were sandy colour in patches and the vegetation was shrub with no trees. The towns of Hong Kong (Princetown and Kowloon) lay to the East.

The towns were a mass of buildings with little or no plan. All were flat topped and some (e.g., The Shanghai and Hong Kong Bank) were of almost skyscraper height and imposing appearance. The main streets were no wider than our side roads. Considering the masses of trishaws, rickshaws, bicycles, cars and pedestrians it was surprising any progress could be made through them.

I had wandered round Kowloon on my day of arrival and had marvelled at the colossal wealth in the shops. The gold, red and blue hues of the silks were remarkable. The teak chests, the jade, the Buddhas and lastly but perhaps being in greatest abundance, the modern watches. One could walk a mile or so of the main street of Kowloon and never be pestered. This was so unlike my experience in Port Said.

This was the end of the line as far as the ship was concerned and all the cargo had been removed from the holds. The rubbish at the bottom known as "dunnage" was being cleaned up by Chinese women with brooms. All over the ship were various types of engineers and electricians doing maintenance work – bearing in mind that the ship was 41 years old it was not surprising. I had done my little bit by examining the new members of the crew for their fitness. At this stage there were conjectures about where we were going next. The general feeling was that we would go to the Philippines and then Borneo, returning home via Singapore. Also at this time many of us talked about the next voyage. I favoured Australia and then America. It was all very hypothetical at this stage.

In the event we did go to the Philippines to pick up copra. The two ports where this took place were on the island of Mindanao, Cebu and Takloban. The latter was famous during the Second World War because the American navy destroyed a Japanese force nearby.

What was not said was that 27,000 US troops and 100,000 Philippines died in this attack. Sixty Japanese ships were sunk.

Copra is the flesh of the coconut and is used to make vegetable oil and margarine. The copra was put in all the holds and my interest in it was that my dispensary was next to a full hold of copra. Unfortunately copra is very attractive to a vicious beetle that looks rather like a Colorado beetle. These beetles were everywhere and soon got into my Dettol in which I kept my so-called sterile syringe. In order to give a full description of them to the folks back home I sent one in a letter. The risk of Colorado beetle affecting potatoes at home had made people aware of this beetle and when the copra bug flew out of the envelope the family chased it round the room until they had killed it!

I got a surprise from the Captain when he said that he had been authorised to give me £20! I assumed that my mention of the cost of goods and my penury had had an effect on my parents. The result of

The author carrying coconuts in Taklotan.

this windfall was a trip ashore to buy more tinned foodstuffs unobtainable in the U K and a suit, a so-called "Palm Beach" light beige linen one. This was made in one day and cost me £5, and after a week's wear looked like a bag!

Before we left the Philippines we had our monthly ritual, which was the Board of Trade games. This was a boat drill which involved us all getting into lifeboats and being lowered over the side into the water and making a few strokes with the oars before being brought back on board. On one memorable occasion as we got half way down and passing the exit hole of a toilet it decided to discharge its contents much to our annoyance. The purpose of the exercise was, of course, to prepare us for the abandonment of the ship.

When we left there were only 15 tons of cargo space out of the 14,000 tons capacity.

Except for coaling in Aden we kept going non-stop for home. One of the most impressive sights was the sunset over the China Seas. This was like the colours of the rainbow slowly changing.

The purser cum wireless operator was a Welshman called Hughes. He was a great lineshooter and constantly pulled my leg about how the ship was run. The latest taunt was his use of my middle name, which he must have found through my passport. After bitter experience I found that silence was the only safe way to react to taunts since the boredom on a ship led to many attempts at getting someone's goat.

I got my own back in finding his hidden name which I enjoyed using when he taunted me. Names were not used on a ship. First, second, third, fourth etc, Mate, Chief (chief engineer), Doc – titles only. It made life very impersonal.

The second mate and the second engineer were my particular friends and it was with them that I usually went ashore. Our favourite occupation was liar dice .We occasionally gambled for a round of drinks and since our tipple on board was ginger beer at 3 pence a bottle they were not very big stakes.

The South West monsoon caused quite a diversion since the wind made it necessary to keep all doors and portholes shut. Despite the strong wind the ship slowly rolled and pitched. Nevertheless walking to my dispensary was a hazardous journey since the waves came over the complete length of the ship. A pleasant relaxation was to lie on a deck chair wearing swimming trunks with eyes shut. Most of the time there was spume but now and then a "green" one came over and drenched me. Other than this the main excitements had been seeing flying fish, some of which came on board and were good eating, the Chief Engineer's cat having five kittens in his drawer, and us siting one ship.

Loading cargo in Taklotan.

I was reminded as we went past Penang that on the way out I had been told by the Captain that at a place called Klang quite close to Port Swettenham I would be able to see rubber trees. In the event I walked for an hour and a half and did eventually see trees and was able to scrape some latex off one to confirm that it was a rubber tree. On the way I saw a Malay funeral procession and heard the firecrackers that would ward off the evil spirits. It was nothing like as impressive as the Chinese funerals with the colours and the dragons in the procession.

Exercise was a problem on a cargo ship and the walking up and down the fore deck was the only one available. I reckoned that 22 times was about three-quarters of a mile. Games of deck quoits could be counted as exercise but the hazards of winches and the rolling of the ship confined it to quiet days.

Reading was of course a major occupation and I got through five Shakespeare plays in ten days.

The variety of drinks had varied from time to time. When we had a hole in the water tank we drank a mixture of sea and fresh water. Now we were on to Export Guinness having finished the ginger beer and lemonade. The atmosphere in the mess when we were drinking this was more congenial than usual, to say the least! Water was one of the most important commodities for a coal burner and only in certain ports was it available in the quantities that we required. At Port Said and Penang water was acceptable but others less so.

The boiler tubes had become partially blocked due to bad coal and had reduced our speed to nine knots. Despite being 50 miles from land we had had a sandstorm that covered the ship in sand. At Aden we picked up a Scottish doctor missionary who had been working twelve miles inland from Aden. He was so virtuous that we all felt constrained to mind our manners. Oddly enough we were expecting to pick up another doctor at Port Said.

In Port Said I bought a pair of white shorts for £1. On a coal burner it was allowed to wear khaki shorts and shirts because of the dirt but on the way home through the Med everyone tried to spruce up a bit and get ready for home.

The seamen were often employed banging on the decks with

The 'cleaned' SS Antilochus.

sledgehammers to remove rust. Rest was impossible whilst this was in progress. However everyone was happy and there was a noticeable change in attitudes when Gibraltar was passed. In Merchant Navy circles this was known as "getting the Channels", in other words getting the feeling that home was very near. "Make and mend" and packing occupied more time and there was more joshing and joking. Many ex service men compared it to being "Demob happy".

So when Liverpool came into sight and welcomes were the order of the day thoughts of the Antilochus were replaced with thoughts of a soft big bed and a visit to an English pub.

It is interesting to record that in 1948 SS Antilochus was sold to the British Iron & Steel Company and on April 11th she was taken to Buton Ferry where she was broken up by Thos. W. Ward.

CHAPTER TWO
SS Arawa

SS Arawa.

An ambition at the start of my National Service, as I thought of it then, was to see as much of the world as possible. For this reason I studied the shipping adverts in the press to see whether I could get to Australia and New Zealand. The opportunity arose to join the SS Arawa, a cargo/passenger ship going round the world and calling at both these places. This was to leave in a month or so. I joined it.

After having the adventure of travelling on an ancient coal burner out to the Far East I felt in need of some comfort and company.

As a result I joined Shaw Savill and Albion's passenger/cargo ship – S S Arawa. In my first short note home that I wrote when we arrived in Southampton, was that she was a "beautiful" ship. Certainly after the Antilochus almost any ship would be beautiful! She was used as an armed Merchant Cruiser and converted to a troop ship in 1941. Her distinction on Tyneside was that she was the second largest passenger ship built there - the largest being the Cunard's Mauretania.

On the Arawa there was a proper surgery, a small ward for four patients, a female nurse, a male attendant and a well-appointed cabin for me.

There was even a garden café and a gymnasium with mechanical horses. So after a good look round the ship we sailed from Liverpool on Friday August 8th to Southampton. On the following day we set sail for Las Palmas. My sick berth attendant was ex R A M C, which meant he knew what to do. He told me that there were twenty children on board so we might be busy if the sea got rough. I opened the dispensary and found that already I had two private patients – both had long standing orthopaedic problems.

Time passed pleasantly enough with a dance in the evening. However the listing of the ship made dancing somewhat difficult. As with the Antilochus I was required to go on inspections This involved the Captain. In addition I had to go on inspections with the Purser to look at passengers' accommodation to see if it was adequate

The number of private patients was increasing but I was not finding any difficulties with the treatments. It was a strict rule that any illness or injury occurring on the voyage and not associated with a previous condition would not be charged. However many of the passengers, particularly the older ones were on medicaments for existing conditions and they all came to me to continue treatment and, of course, were charged for each visit.

The weather was gorgeous and much of the day was spent sunbathing or playing deck tennis. The swimming pool was now in operation but few used it. The 300 or so passengers found plenty to occupy their time. There was a film show most nights and the one I attended was unusual in that there was a defect in the reels, which caused jumping and sticking!

The swimming pool.

Shooting stars were a great attraction at night-time.

On the 14th of August we arrived at Las Palmas in the Canary Islands. We were only there a day and left at 4 in the afternoon. There was only time to have a look around the shops in the town. The sea was calm but the weather was hot and sticky. I was introduced to a massive Pyrenean Mountain dog whose owner was going to use it as a gimmick to advertise his business in Melbourne. It was bigger than a St Bernard and I was told the strain was over 2000 years old. Its back legs were longer than its front ones which made sense if it had to climb mountains! We were shown a photo of the dog with its front paws on the shoulders of its master !

During the day there had been a competition guessing the distance we would travel in 24 hours and the winner got a certificate.

The entertainment in the evening varied. There was a film, a dance, a bingo session or a race meeting. The latter involved betting on horses that were moved according to the throw of a dice. Some of the passengers were going to Australia on the assisted passage scheme with the intention of emigrating there. One pair were professional dancers and they gave an exhibition dance one night.

On Sunday there was a church service for all denominations. By this means one could tell what day of the week it was! Inevitably there were minor squabbles when boredom set in and the cramped cabin conditions made occupants complain of the congestion and request a transfer to a larger cabin.

As one would expect the meals were far too lavish for the very sedentary life style and five course dinners had to be severely pruned to avoid a massive increase in weight. We were making for Cape Town and ways of making the days interesting were exercising the purser's ingenuity. A Fancy Dress dance was one of the ideas that caused not only a great deal of thought but improvisation. Those passengers who enjoyed classical music were not missed out in that there was a concert with records of Tchaikowsky.

On the 27th of August we arrived in Cape Town and everyone was thrilled to see the top of Table Mountain with its "table cloth" covering it. I went to the best hotel in the city – the Mount Nelson – where I was entertained until the small hours by one of the passengers who got off here. Inevitably the following day I went to the summit of Table Mountain. It was fortunate that it was a clear day and the views were spectacular. In all my travels I felt that this city had everything to commend it --a superb climate, wonderful surroundings and a happy population.

So after two days in Cape Town we set sail for Melbourne across the Indian Ocean and the Roaring Forties. The latter was where big waves roll across with tremendous troughs. Not frightening when in a reasonably sized ship but nevertheless awe-inspiring. Often accompanying us would be an albatross with a sixteen-foot wingspan. It would hardly move its wings but soar effortlessly above. Due to the Roaring Forties and the rolling and pitching of the ship I was kept busy looking after the many seasick passengers. Since this was part of the hazards of the voyage I could not count these treatments as private and so could not charge for the treatment.

There were various spin offs from bad weather conditions. There were many less at meals. Meals themselves were somewhat of an adventure since to get to one's table one had to stagger across the room and probably hit someone's table. Having sat down there would be "fiddles" around the edges of the table. These strips of wood stopped plates sliding off but despite them there were inevitably many accidents. The worst of these was a bowl of hot soup landing on one's lap!

This weather made the ship go faster and we were going at over 15 knots, which was about our maximum. We also covered 350 miles in a day, which was also a record.

Though the loss of crockery was quite a problem more seriously was the danger of cargo shifting. Many horrendous stories were told of ships being overturned by cargoes, particularly bulk, shifting. Ours was well packed in the holds and did not cause any problems. However my dispensary was a shambles with bottles broken on the floor. In the kitchen a bacon slicer worth £120 fell and broke. I was kept busy looking after patients with bruises.

A rather distasteful job I had to do was to kill off cats with chloroform. The reason was that for every unregistered (i.e. not on the ship's list of animals on board) cat that got ashore the ship would be fined £50.

Now the weather was sunny and the sea much calmer. Once again deck games became popular. At this stage in the voyage a change was noticed in the mood of passengers. Perhaps they had been away from proper civilization for too long but some passengers tended to be critical of each other and there were some slanderous remarks made.

On the 16th of August we arrived in Melbourne. The first thing I had to do was to take a patient up to the main hospital in Melbourne. This lady had caught her head a severe blow when getting into a taxi in Cape Town and had a painful neck and symptoms suggesting that she might have damaged her spinal chord. I had kept her lying down during the voyage across the Indian Ocean with sandbags to keep her neck immobile. At the super £2,000,000 hospital she was immediately investigated. I left her there whilst I was taken on a tour of the hospital and then the city. On returning I was told that there was no neurological damage and with physiotherapy she would soon be back to normal. I took her back to the ship and got the nurse to massage her neck and start exercises.

The following day we left Melbourne for Wellington, New Zealand. Soon everyone left was starting packing since Wellington was the end of the line. I tried to get my fees for my private patient consultations but sometimes was unsuccessful! I made about £50 on this outward voyage.

We arrived in Wellington on the 22nd of August – the weather staying sunny all the time despite the reputation of the Tasman Sea being notoriously poor. Once again I went to the local hospital but not to take a patient, purely to make myself known and look around. My lady with the stiff neck had managed to walk ashore on her own I was pleased to say.

I spoke to the Shaw Savill office manager in Wellington and tried to

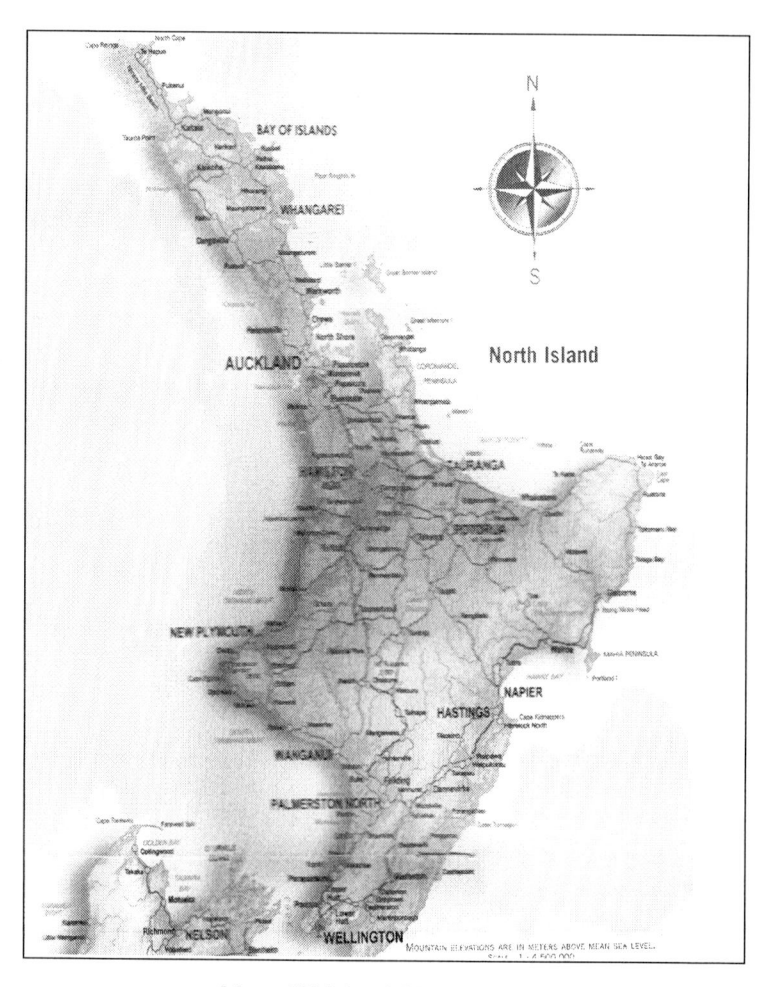

Map of N.Island, New Zealand.

get permission to take some leave so that I could tour North Island. This was more difficult than I thought it would be and so many restrictions were put on me including that if there were any accidents and the company had to pay medical fees I would have had to pay them. I gave up this approach and went to the Captain who gave me permission.

So on the 26th I went off by Service Car, which was like a small charabanc to Rotorua. We took the coast road through Levin stopping at Palmerston North for lunch. Since it was Spring the grass was very green. The land rugged. The mountain ranges made the roads difficult It felt we were twisting and turning to get to the top or go to the bottom of mountains. Cinder tracks and no guards on the side of the roads made the journey exciting. The alternative to road travel would be rail but since the gauge was only 3 ft. 6 ins. this would be quite uncomfortable. The type of terrain also meant that the trains were very slow.

The AA had done sterling work in putting up signs. One would see "Give way one car bridge" and "Engage second gear deceptive gradient" or "Try your brakes" after we had gone through a water splash. When there was a sign saying "Dangerous corner" the driver took notice! Also when the sign said, "Go slow – you have been warned!" the driver invariably took notice. 90% of the dwellings were bungalows made of wood and painted white. They all had tiled or painted galvanized iron roofs. The impression was of neatness and cleanliness. There were two reasons for wooden bungalows. The main one was the abundance of timber the other was the frequency of earthquakes, which though not severe would upset a brick building.

The towns rather reminded me of the Wild West in old American movies. Usually there was a main street and in the case of Palmerston North the railway ran down the centre of this street. So when an express went through the whole town shook. All the stores had gables and roofs that overhung the sidewalk. Everything seemed happy – go - lucky and I could honestly say I had never met a more congenial community than in these towns. A political grumble might be voiced but they certainly had a good time.

I had lunch there and was introduced to whitebait. Here it was tiny string like fish quite unlike the sort one meets at home. It was delicious in an omelette. Meat was rationed and often but not always, one was asked for a coupon if one had beef or other meat.

From Palmerston North we went alongside the Ruakine Range where we at last saw a few sheep on the hillsides. The mountains were covered in scrub, which looked very untidy to my English eyes. Bearing in mind that there were less than 2 million people in this land it was understandable that there was little in the way of tidying the countryside. We then entered Napier, which had a nasty earthquake in 1931 It was as dead as a Dodo after 6pm ! Pubs shut then and it was usual for drinkers to line up their drinks on the counter and when the bell went at 6 p.m. to down them quickly, The result was a sight of staggering drunks soon after 6pm ! There was one show in the cinema at 8 p.m. That was the excitement of the town. Roller-skating on the promenade seemed to be the only entertainment during the day.

   I stayed the night in the Marine Drive Hotel. The proprietor told me about the earthquake and showed me two panoramic photographs taken before and after. The effect was similar to Hiroshima's atom bomb. Many lives were lost and many bodies were never recovered. Although devastating there was one good effect It made the sea recede and brought marshy land up and this was now good pasture. Talking to him about the effects on people of an earthquake he said that he had met some who were mentally affected by the incident.

   I went to a film that was called appropriately "The Beginning or the End" which was about the dropping of the atom bomb! It was the usual American blab and served only to pass the time.

   On Thursday I went from Napier to Rotorua leaving at 8am. Being a democrat I sat next to three female Maoris. I got talking to the one next to me and she told me she was from Rotorua and was a guide at their village of Whakarewarewa (try and pronounce that!) Hearing that I was the doctor of the Arawa, which was the name of her tribe she took me under her wing. That evening she arranged for me to go to the pictures with her niece, Elsie – 4 feet 6 inches high and aged 21! Rangi was world famous and I was honoured that she called me Peter. She was well spoken and had met crowned heads of Europe. The Duke of Windsor, the Duke of Gloucester, Mrs Roosevelt, (remember a prize winning photograph of Mrs R rubbing noses with Rangi?) Gracie Fields and recently George Formby came round with her. I had got into a medium sized hotel called the Charms but as it was raining when I got to Rotorua I didn't look far as I hadn't got a mac.

   Later that night I met a fellow called Desmond Burrows, (who looked like Lou Costello, the small American film comic) He said the Maoris were a dirty race and in order to prove it took me to a village dance at Ohinimatu about a mile from Rotorua. We watched through the stained glass window of the meetinghouse. He couldn't show me any scabby legs, etc. so I reserved judgement!

The following day I went on a Government Round Tour of the lakes. The Government was very efficient as far as tours, etc were concerned and I think if we had the same system at home it would be a very prolific source of internal revenue.

In order to get the right idea about the "thermal area" as it was called an explanation is necessary. Firstly New Zealand's North Island was in the earthquake belt that stretches from America to Japan. Thus the whole country was liable (except Waiatomo Caves – more of that later) to quakes of varying severity or tidal waves, as at Gisborne three or four years ago. Thermal areas however were found also in Greenland and Colorado. It was all very uncanny.

In 1886 on June 10th Mount Tarawera started erupting followed rapidly by two other volcanoes close by. It killed 200 people at once and buried a whole village in larva. Strangely enough this volcano belt could be seen right across the island starting at White Island in the Bay of Plenty (the only constantly erupting volcano in the world) across Tarawera and Rainbow Mountain (famous because the explosion exposed all the strata and the colours from white to red) to Mount Egmont (N.Z.'s Fujiyama).

One could not conceive what had happened or was happening under Rotorua. On the route we saw first of all a deep crater, one third filled with water. The water never varies in level and was acid and normal temperature. Nothing will live in it at all. About a quarter of a mile away was what was known as a frying pan flat. It was a lake of a beautiful blue with a brown edge and it was boiling! The depth had not been estimated, as it was too hot to keep the boat on it.

Eruption of Tarawera volcano, 1886.

About 100 yards away was the site of the Wimanga Geyser. This used to blow off every 36 hours to a height of 1,500 feet but on April 1st 1917 (note – April Fools day!) , while a crowd of tourists were waiting in a special hut for it to blow off, it gave its last and biggest. This time it reached 1,500 feet with its first spout but for the first and last time it gave another gigantic shower of steam, boulders and larva to a height of 2,500 feet!

The tragedy was that four people who had not seen the geyser before had deserted the party and had hidden behind a rock only a couple of hundred yards away. Their bodies were found a mile down the valley. As it was April Fools day the doctor thought the whole thing a hoax when he was called to the aid of people in a house half a mile from the explosion.

Further on was a most beautiful terrace effect due to the warm and heavy silica and iron content in the water. The playing fountain of warm water on circular sloping terraces with all the colours of the rainbow in streaks had to be seen to be believed.

Then to Lake Rotomahana where we went on a launch trip past the bird sanctuary and the steaming cliffs (steam and bubbling water) Cygnets got caught in the backwash and it would appear they would be scalded but no – they just fluttered into the cooler water and seemed unharmed. Rotomahana itself was the youngest lake in the world. It appeared after the 1886 explosion. The shores all the way round were corrugated like the top of a corrugated iron roof. This was all mud from the explosion. We walked to Lake Tarawera and got another launch across it. From there we went by coach to Te Wairoa Falls and a Maori village, which had been completely covered by the mud from the bang.

The next part of the journey showed the amazing changes in the colour of the water in two lakes only separated by a couple of yards. One lake was a definite blue and higher by a foot or so than the other, which was, green! The reason was to be found in the colour of the lake bottom. Then back to Rotorua.

After tea I had a hot thermal bath in the Blue Baths near by. Some of these hotels never had a fire or electricity or gas for heating. The hot (sometimes 230 F superheated, because of the mineral impurities) water was used (a) in pipes to warm cold clean water or (b) directly as central heating or (c) the Maoris had grates in the ground with iron bars on which they put all their food. It was possible to catch a trout in one pool and without moving and still on the line cook it in another pool!

Anyway to return I had a hot 98 F bath. The smell was of hydrogen sulphide (bad eggs) but it was pleasant swimming around in it. Other baths were up to 100 F. or were mud, radium, etc. It all came from the ground via pipes and the Government made some money from it.

In the evening I went with Des, to a Maori-cum-White dance at the Meeting House. This was a wooden hall with Maori carved effigies on the walls and at the entrance. Maori musicians hit out the rhythms but unfortunately my creepers (crepe soled shoes) made it difficult for me to dance, but I got around. I met some of the nurses from the local hospital. Everyone was much less formal and friendlier than at home. The first thing a New Zealander did was to ask you your name and immediately called you by your first name. We never did that at home.

Saturday was without doubt the most crowded day of my life!

At 9 a.m. I went up in a De Havilland Tiger Moth with my friend on a half hour trip round the Rotoura district. It was a perfect morning. We could see from White Island to Mount Egmont, right across the width of the country. As the route was similar to the one yesterday I was able to really appreciate the views. My friend felt airsickness but only held the paper bag without doing anything but change colour!

At 10 a.m. I went on a tour of Whaka (short for Whakarewarewa!) with Rangi who singled me out to see around her home and sign in her own book on the same page as George Formby of Hale, Cheshire. The sights of Whaka were the cooking arrangements in the ground using steam or hot water. There was no taint to food according to Rangi. Other things of interest were the geysers. The Prince of Wales feathers was one of them – these were three jets at different angles. It played precociously and we were lucky to see it. Snowy silica terraces (pure white and covered in boiling water), mud pools (very amusing as the grey mud was a hive of activity) One pool was called the 'frog pool' and the steam came up so rapidly that the mud jumped like a frog. Another pool was called 'Rose' or 'Tulip' as the mud lifted up and formed petals very like a flower.

Also at this village was a complete native "Pa" which was Maori for village. I saw the carvings (done laboriously by Rangi's Grandfather) and the native huts, canoes, etc. An interesting feature of Whaka was that all graves in the graveyard were above the ground and were kept warm by the earth – as Rangi said "no one could say - Papa's in the cold, cold snow!"

After this we got in the car, picked up an Australian (by the way Des B was a New Zealander) called Ian Smith whom I met in the baths and we went to Waiotapu. We went unguided despite the fact we paid 2 shillings! However we saw all sorts of wonders. Craters frightening in their dangerous, rumbling, boiling state and an unsettling hollow feeling on treading the paths made you think of Dante's Inferno. Each crater had a peculiar colour or smell. The oxides of iron and various sulphides gave colours from a gloomy black to brown, red, yellow and blue. It was uncanny how one could put one's hand into a pool of clear drinkable cold water then put it into (if foolish enough!) a boiling hot black smelly one a few feet away.

Des could not get over the frying pan lake here, which was covered in steam and was a beautiful blue. Round its edges iron oxides had built up to form a red ledge and as the rock around was white it looked quite technicoloured. A favourite sport was to throw pumice into the water and get the champagne effect of bubbles coming up. Des, again, who was a small boy at heart, got bigger and bigger stones until we feared he would reach an untimely end by not letting go!

The lovely colours despite the fact that the smell was a little "off" were remarkable even after all we had seen. Next we moved on to the Aratiatia Rapids where Des who owns a yacht up in Auckland spent a fruitful half an hour collecting pumice rocks for sandpapering its hull. They (i.e. the rapids) were no better than Betwys-y-Coed in Wales but still for this country it showed a contrast to the previous experiences.

On to Wairakei where we had to get in by lifting the gate off its hinges, as the guides only work a 40-hour week (the big grumble out here). We wandered along a valley full of geysers and bubbling hot springs terraces and coloured pools. These geysers could be timed to the minute and it was uncanny to sit down and watch one go off every two minutes by the clock.

On to Karopiti Blow Hole, which again necessitated a removal of a gate and a half-mile, walk through the bush. This was different from anything up to date. I held on to a long (12 foot) heavy plank and placed one end over the blasting orifice of the hole and lifted the other end. The plank was lifted to the horizontal. A penny (or even a half-crown) thrown in would be tossed out and almost unbearably hot. Imagine this power used to drive a turbine!

From there we went on to Lake Taupo as the sun was setting. We had a very quick dinner. All three of us were much bespattered and very hungry but in this country a usual dinner was soup, steak, with two eggs and onions, sweet and coffee. Des's small 1934 Austin 7 got us back from Taupo to Rotorua in an hour and a quarter, a distance of 38 miles, which was miraculous considering the bumpy road.

At 8.45 p.m. without changing I went straight to a Maori Concert (Rangi organized it for me – so she said). Here again I had a new experience. The Maori seemed generally to be a happy people despite the fact that there was the odd remote Maori camp in the darkest parts of New Zealand where head hunting on a small scale was still carried out.

Their smiles and fat bodies in grass and beaded skirts gave the dances a happy atmosphere. The "Haka" or "War dance" was one in which everyone got very excited and the men put their tongues out to one side and roll their eyes up to the other side! Much stamping and gesticulating made you glad that you were on their side. Then came the Poi dancing. This was the most rhythmical dance I had ever seen. In each hand the line of girls had a type of grass ball on the end of a piece of grass. To the music they revolve these balls swaying their bodies in unison. The balls went to and fro twisting one way and then the other or hitting the backs of the wrists or forearms. The "canoe" Poi dance was performed with two seated lines of girls swaying and twirling their Pois to the rhythm of the chant. It was very lilting and was the nearest thing to a South Sea Island dance I was to see. These Maoris were of course Polynesian and thus were South Sea Islanders.

Various songs were sung to the music from a very honky-tonk piano. Lastly they sang the sad farewell song. This was without doubt the most moving of all , especially when sung by Maoris. When we got back to the hotel Ian suggested that we go to the Soda Springs near Rotorua for a moonlit bathe. I accepted and lo and behold we find our youthful adventurer lying in a stream in about two feet of warm water at 2a.m. under a moonlit starry sky. The experience capped all for that day and I certainly had not lacked any. The water was warm enough for a few minutes, then a hot stream would preponderate and I had to shift about six inches one way, so that I could get into the cool part. I was lying at the confluence of a hot and a cold stream. What a day!

Sunday Sept. 28th was when I went to the stream where I had bathed earlier in the morning. The lakes were lovely in sunlight, even lovelier than by moonlight. The visual contrasts in this country were quite bewildering, mountains, rivers, lakes, volcanoes, thermal activity, and lovely forests. Then to Tikitere the place that George Bernard Shaw said he would have given £5 not to have seen! The guide tried to turn it into an advert but failed miserably as it was so blatantly true! It was drab, grey sulphurous boiling mud. It made you wish you could be an honest citizen even if it was difficult. This was such as I imagined.

In the afternoon we went to Orakai Korako. This was the most beautiful drive of the whole trip. The Waikato River and the wooded mountains made the scene perfect. It looked, as I would expect Canada to be. Although it was forty miles the Austin 7 managed it all right, keeping up forty miles an hour all the way.

A great disappointment awaited us there as the manager told us the Government were surveying the ferry, which took tourists across the river to the actual thermal area. After a lot of "line shooting" I was able to persuade him to take us across in a rowing boat about an hour later.

In the meantime we continued up the valley in the car, the track narrowed and we got into the true native bush with trees pressing on both sides. A couple of dogs followed us all the way, biting at the tyres and barking at us. After about three miles on a really bumpy cart track and after having forded two quite deep water splashes we found ourselves miles away from anywhere with no immediate prospect of getting anywhere. So we turned back and met the manager again who was ready to take us across the fast flowing river.

We were taken the hundred and fifty yards in a very flimsy small rowing boat, one at a time. We then saw the sights. At Orakai Korako the main accent was on colour and the guide who really was interested in the chemical side of the business gave us some idea of the formation of the beautiful colours. Each pool was different from the next and unlike most other pools I had seen they had clear water. Here again we saw terraces that stretched sideways for about two hundred yards.

The surprising thing about the look of these formations was that you could swear it was soft to walk on, but no, it was absolutely solid. The tones of the colours at this particular place were due to the algae, which grew in large numbers in hot, and in fewer numbers in cold water.

Geysers of varying ferocity were shown to us. Some were precocious and despite the guide's curses would not play! It was very tantalizing to see one just about to play but suddenly stop only to play when you were just out of sight. Many times we heard one and had to dash at great speed back on our tracks to find it had stopped in the meantime.

After the morning at Tikitere where everything was dingy this was an enchantingly pleasant change and we were so impressed with the colours that we asked if James A Fitzpatrick the famous travel talks technicolour film man had been there. The reply was that his outfit had been overturned in the river while crossing with the result that he had to be rescued from a rock only a short distance from the rapids. He had only three days in New Zealand at that time so he couldn't do any filming but he had the good fortune to fall in love with one of the party who came to Orakai Koro. He subsequently married her. He said he was coming back.

Des had a date at 8 p.m. so we made yet another of those lightning flashes back to base. He went out but soon returned with two Maoris, who, he said, were inseparable and would I escort him. This I did but the evening was not successful as we both had had about a hundred miles of back jolting Austin riding and the prospect of a sight - seeing moonlight tour was uncomfortable to say the least. So the evening was short as Des said we should go to Wiotapu for beer and if we couldn't get any we would go home. As pubs shut at 6 p.m. and there were no off – licences, or even a bit of graft, I was in bed for 10 p.m.

On Monday, fortunately, I had met a chappie at a dance at Ohinimutu who had offered me a ride up to Auckland in his car. I had accepted. The man's name I think was Mac. It later turned out that he was a traffic 'cop'. It was unfortunate in a way because his Ford 10 could have kept up a steady 50 but he wouldn't go over 40 on country roads and 30 in towns since these were the speed limits! After Des's mad driving with a smaller car it soon palled.

I had wanted to see the Fairy Springs that were famous trout pools close to Rotorua. You would not credit it but I actually fed the trout (not captive trout) with bread and they bit my fingers. With a little effort I was able to catch hold of them and lift them out of the water! The maximum weight of a trout caught in this area was over 325 pounds at Lake Taupo. The ones I saw were no more than 18 pounds.

That was the last scenic claim on Rotorua and everyone said I had not missed much. Everyone at the Charms had been kindness itself and when the weather got cold I was offered coupons to get clothes. I bought a sweater but the shopkeeper wouldn't accept the coupons. Numerous people talked to me, the sole subject of conversation being how things were doing at home and what were the best things to send to England.

This fellow Mac and I went to Auckland at a leisurely pace stopping for a steak, eggs and onions lunch at the pleasant farming town of Hamilton. This place also had a railway running through it. The country round about had sheep and cattle with miles and miles of grazing land. The game in these parts was a great attraction to the sportsman. Unlike in England you could get out of the car and take a rifle (Mac had a .22 rifle in the back of the car) and shoot deer, pig, rabbit or wild goats without a licence or any bother about preservation. They were all considered vermin. This country was full of outdoor sports i.e. fishing, shooting, winter sports such as skiing (South Island particularly, but also in the Tongauro National Park, North Island), climbing and yachting. All were very well patronized. Horseracing and rugby were the national sports. But as I said before they had few interests other than sport.

We arrived in Auckland at 4 p.m. and I immediately got in touch with a Mr Owen Barrett who was a great friend of Des. He took me up Mount Eden just before the sun went down. From there one could get an uninterrupted view of all the bays and suburbs of Auckland. Owen told me that a German sub had been only a few miles away and had flown its plane over Auckland during the war. This piece of panic-producing news had only recently been published.

I stayed the night at the Grosvenor Hotel that was not very pretentious but as it was raining I didn't bother looking around for a better one. I had a meal at a local café of suckling pig. It was really succulent and very like chicken.

In the evening I went to the Orange Grove Hall where Owen plays the piano (a spare time hobby) and danced with some of the locals. The amazing thing about Kiwis was that they were all one class and you could talk to anyone and find that socially they were all equal. Class distinction was almost unknown. I was not sure whether I liked it!

Having had a walk around Auckland and gaining a general impression of the size, and the types of buildings etc. I got the 8 a.m. service car to Waiatomo caves which was in what was called the "King" county. Here there was a regulation that no alcohol could be served.

Unfortunately it was a very wet day but I got to the Waiatomo Hostel by lunchtime. The caves were in the middle of lovely sheep country, well wooded and about six miles from the nearest shop at Hangatiki on the main Hamilton to New Plymouth road.

This hostel was Governmentally controlled and had the tourist trade well organized. I was able to see the three caves, Ruakuri, Aranui, and the Waiatomo (glow-worm) on the same day. The guide had the usual patter, rather like a small child rushing through a recitation that you almost had the feeling that any moment he would say, " Can I have the piece of cake now, Mummy? " at the end of it.

The Ruakuri cave was shabby. The only startling parts were the underground river and some stalactites and stalagmites, which I told him, were generally better in the Cheddar caves. The lighting was harsh with naked bulbs not placed appropriately to give the best effect.

He agreed with all this. This area was associated with Maori legends and history that was fascinating to hear.

The Aranui cave was better and the party had grown a bit by then. The guide kept on pointing to 'mites' that had a vague resemblance to people. About 5% of the crowd saw the resemblance but no one gave an appreciative "Ah" or "Oh" to boost up the guide's ego. The only one that I felt was worthy of comment was that of George Bernard Shaw. When he, during a visit to the cave, was shown this he was reputed to have said, "It shows how important I must be. They had thought of me thousands of years ago!" When it is considered that it took 400 years for a cubic inch of 'mite" or 'tite" to form, the estimated age of the 10 feet columns was beyond comprehension.

This part was not subject to earthquakes and the last one was 3600 years ago – so the guide told us. The colours were less drab in this cave but my previous criticisms still held. Gough's caves in Derbyshire were much more commercialised. These caves could be as good if they were developed.

Lastly after dinner at 7.30 pm we went to the glow-worm cave. Now this one event transcended all the others. It was so overpowering that it left everyone speechless. The glow-worm is the larva of a fly. It was shaped like a little worm in a slimy cradle. They measured up to 5 inches in length. Most of the body had no luminosity, It was in the rear that the glow emanated In the front of the body hung up to twenty threads that could be up to 2 feet in length. They were sensitive to air movement and therefore sound. Sound causes the glow to reduce. These glow-worms are found nowhere else in the world. No-one knows why.

They were all on the roof – millions of them densely crammed together. The mechanism was that the glow – worm had a chemical in its tail segments that gave off a blue colour but no heat. This attracted small flies that hit the threads and got stuck to them. The glow – worm then hauled on the appropriate thread and ate the fly. It then drops a new thread to replace the used one. So when we talked some of the lights went out and a sudden bang caused most of them to go out. Similarly a bright light had the same effect.

We went into the cave and saw all the other attractions such as the "cathedral" that was renowned for its acoustic properties. Here Gracie Fields sang and later annoyed Monte Banks (her husband) by coming back from her car to try out another song down there. Broadcasts have been held down there. The guide sang to give us a good idea. A Yank in the party could only show his appreciation by uttering "For Pete's sake!" It wasn't clear whether this appreciation was for the singing or the spectacle. The Yank was clearly drunk and in view of the teetotal nature of the King county I wondered if he had a hip flask!

We saw some fine examples of 'tites' and 'mites' The way to tell which was a stalactite and which was a stalagmite was that when the tites come down the mites go up! So the guide told us. We got into a large rowing boat and with many "Oohs" and "Ahs" and "For Pete's sake" the unearthly canopy of millions of glow-worms were seen.

I had never seen such an awe-inspiring sight. Not another word was uttered during this short voyage round this underground lake. The guide used a wire above the boat to pull it around the lake. Constellations of glow-worms would show up as we went around. As this lake was continuous with a stream outside it was essential that the cavern was in darkness for the glow-worms to glow. After that great sight I did not expect to see anything so wonderful. It was just as well as the weather broke that night and it rained nearly all the time on our journey down to New Plymouth where I stayed on the Wednesday night.

New Plymouth was famous because of its close proximity to Mount Egmont, a large solitary extinct volcano. As the weather was so bad I was unable to see it and after spending the night at the White Hart Hotel I went on to Wellington. I met the Auckland commercial traveller for a big Sheffield cutlery company. He advised me on the easy way to buy Royal Doulton china whilst out here. This was of importance to me because my mother collected this ware.

The journey down was uneventful and not very interesting as I had seen it on the way north.

When I got back to the ship I heard that there had been nothing in the medical line to do until the Tuesday night when two men had fallen down a hold resulting in one breaking his neck and the other breaking his leg. I went up to the hospital each day after I got back and watched progress. It was very sad that the boy with the broken neck though conscious was paralysed below the arms. He was to be 21 this weekend. His mate was not in such a dangerous state though his fracture was compound.

The last three days were spent either at the hospital or on the ship with the exception of the last Saturday night when I went to the Majestic cabaret.

It had been quite an anticlimax after the adventurous nine days to sit down and have nothing to see or hear. I had got to know one or two doctors up at the hospital but until the following day I could not start seeing cases. Fortunately the Director of Medical Services qualified in Manchester in 1901and knew many of my teachers. He extended the whole of the teaching facilities to me whilst I was here.

I went a long walk with the third and fifth mates to a place called Happy Valley about four miles from the port. We followed a stream the hard way by taking our shoes and stockings off and wading. After a mile or so we came across a youth with a fine sieve looking in the water. He told me he was a geology student looking for a type of water snail that would prove that New Zealand and Australia were once one.

This led to a heated denial on my part, which produced masses of evidence to show that NZ was connected to South America. Of course, my opinion was only based on what I had read about the primitive tribes who were related to the Incas, plus none of the animals or reptiles found in Australia. After a few minutes we exchanged chocolates and he made tea. This was made without milk or sugar, which we drank without enthusiasm. It took us a couple of hours to walk back over the hills to the ship.

I mentioned going to the Majestic cabaret. This was the best dance hall in Wellington and on Saturday night, smart dress was compulsory. I went with the second and fifth mates in uniform but the fifth mate's girl friend went in a short dress. We had to seek the manager out before we could enter. It was just hard luck that the numbers meant that I was "odd man out". After the day's hike I was pleased to give my "dogs" a well earned rest! The supper was crayfish. It was a delicacy out here and even though I had had a supper on the ship, oddly enough of crayfish (plus Guinness!), I scoffed it.

Strangely enough, this Puritanical government, thanks to a non-smoking, T.T. Prime Minister prohibits drinking after 6 p.m. and also forbids anyone taking alcoholic drink into a cabaret. Were the clients sober? Not a bit of it! It was amazing where the booze came from and many an embarrassing situation had arisen when a gin or whiskey bottle had dropped out of a highly respectable lady's coat pocket. This narrow-minded bigotry extended to all pleasures on holidays. There was nothing open on Sundays except churches and there were no Sunday newspapers. Taken all round it was an excellent country if you could accept that one had largely to make one's own enjoyment. Culture and sophistication were not yet flourishing. To live in England and have London theatres, concerts and exhibitions, together with the "pubs", was more attractive to me.

One observation of interest to motorists was that many of the cars here were old. The range was from a 1947 American car to a Model T Ford, 1924 Essex, Crystler, De Soto. You could hardly credit your eyes when you saw a farmer coming down the street driving an old jalopy and his son behind him driving a new 1947 super de luxe American vehicle. A 1924 Packard was for sale in Auckland – mileage 24,000, condition as new! Driving here was like I would imagine it was in England prior to the First World War. The clouds of pumice dust cause a great change in the appearance of a car after a mile or two especially in the rain. Many of the roads were single track with an unguarded precipice on either side. This led to only the experienced getting out into the wilds. Fitness tests for cars every six months was routine here. This was a good thing and one that should be introduced into the UK.

Randolph Churchill was in Wellington that weekend. He was unpopular because of his anti-labour views. He was considered a warmonger and no one had a good word to say for him. The headline in the local newspaper was "England's No. 1 Spiv" and under it "Send him home"

We were due to sail on October 17th and so should be home on the 21st of November.

The waterside workers in New Zealand were the uncertain quantity and their 40 hour week and their almost "go slow" policy to turn the ships round at a third of the rate that they do in London. They were a disgrace to the efforts that New Zealand was making to help Britain in her crisis. No one had a good word to say about them and all were ashamed of them. It was "mob rule" – the Unions ruled the government.

The weather was most unpredictable and high winds and driving rain alternated with glorious sunshine.

We were a fortnight behind schedule when we left and as the season for importing mutton from New Zealand was just about to start it meant that the ship would be turned around with all possible speed in the UK. It was expected that the ship would sail outward bound before Christmas!

Five of the crew were in hospital, one with appendicitis, one with bowel trouble, two who fell down the hold, and one who fell off a horse! The case of appendicitis was of particular importance to me. I had diagnosed his condition a few days before but in hospital they had 'sat on' him since they were not sure. Luckily for me he showed real signs of the disease and they operated. I had fears that he would be sent back to the ship and he would flare up at sea with me having to perform the operation without any assistance. I thought that but the

Captain told me that a nursing sister who, according to him, had a naughty twinkle in her eye and was tall, blonde and single would assist me on the home run! Having little experience of women I would have to watch my step !

I went to the Boronowski Ballet Company's production of Swan Lake, Scherazade, le Spectre de la Rose and Cappricio Italien. I surprised myself by thoroughly enjoying it. It was at the Wellington Opera House and like most of the buildings out here was drab.

The first time for at least half a decade I went to a church. This was St Paul's where last Sunday I attended a Trafalgar Day service to commemorate the soldiers lost in the war. Governor General Frieberg was there and all the flags were paraded. The church was drab and made of wood but the seats were comfortable.

I booked a tour of South Island by plane for my last weekend but rain stopped me. A great disappointment since I wouldn't have another opportunity.

When we left New Zealand we only had 133 passengers as no one wants to go to England at this time of the year. This would have been a very satisfactory arrangement if they had been like those outward bound. They were poor both financially and intellectually. They were a peculiar range of ages. Babies of 3 to 18 months associated with young married couples contrasted with the very old that seemed as if they were going home to die. The young ones had little time for socializing since they had to look after their children. Also they were often disappointed with the life in New Zealand and missed the pleasures of home.

Officers had their individual tables and I was lucky in that I had a Surgeon Captain Quinn sitting on my right. He was very "pukkah"

Passengers and the author (left).

and "regular Navy" and very pedantic. An attractive newly wed sat opposite him. I often had fun imitating him. A lady doctor sat on my right. She was over 60 but full of sparkle and despite her spinsterhood had packed many varied experiences into her life.

She related morbid tales of medicine in the raw miles away from anywhere in a her practice at a township 3000 miles from Perth while the Surg Cap'n talked about "Chinah". He was influential in changing our breakfast routine. He was not happy with the chatter at breakfast time. He said in the Royal Navy everyone brought a newspaper or book to the table and beyond a "good morning" all would be quiet. He did not enlarge on this custom but in view of the habits of Naval officers it might well be that this custom was related to helping cure a hangover. Anyway it was agreed and we all brought books to breakfast thereafter. To my left was the daughter of a radiologist in Christchurch. She had a great sense of humour and kept the conversation going at other meal times Also at our table was an elderly, tough-looking man with the most gnarled hands I had ever seen. He had been a deck hand on a sailing ship and because of his large knuckles he could not hold a knife and fork properly. Taciturn was the only word for his conversation! Among the passengers were about a dozen whom you would want to meet socially (that sounds patronizing and perhaps it is!). The rest were typical rural New Zealanders (solid, simple, good folk). At a table near mine was a man with a husky voice and ears like Dumbo. His face was battered and one day he told me his voice had never been the same since Primo Carnera hit him on the larynx in 1929 ! He came in to dinner wearing a pullover and an open necked shirt instead of a suit.

The weather across the Pacific was smooth and the only bit of high wind and sea was when we were near Pitcairn Island. We had a few barrels of oil to deliver there but because of the high seas we were not able to deliver them into their boats. The population's trade was in stamps, which though valued at 4s-7d cost us, 10s.

Then we reached the Panama Canal It was quite an experi-

Pitcairn Island.

A lock in the Panama Canal.

ence to feel the ship lifted up by the water in the locks 85 feet and looking down on the Pacific. It beat the Suez into a cocked hat and the way the Americans got the ship through speedily was remarkable. Most impressive was to see the electrically-powered "mules" pulling the ship through the locks. These "mules" ran on rails and were held on to the ship with hawsers. In the locks it only took 15 minutes for us to go up 29 feet. After each lock 8 mules, four either side would quickly get secured to the ship and start moving it on to the next lock. The mules went up slopes of up to 45 degrees. The locks were cut through the mountains and there was an eerie quiet as we went through with such speed. The only sound we heard was that of a tropical bird.

'Mule' on the bank of the Panama Canal.

The enormity of the task was the thing that stayed in my memory. From the point of view of scenic beauty it was only fair. The weather was fine and so we saw it in ideal conditions. After passing through the Gatum Lake we came down in three steps to the level of the Atlantic. It took eight hours to cover the fifty miles. We got alongside at Christobel which was the port of Colon at 10.30 pm and went ashore.

I had purchased $10 from the lady doctor for £2. That was good business as in Panama the rate of exchange was as low as $2.75 to the £1. A party of twelve of us – all passengers – went ashore first of all to the Coco cabaña, then to the Monte Carlo and finally to the Florida. These nightclubs start very late at night and as the town relies on ships for its custom we were stung well and truly.

At the Coco Cabaña the cabaret was just finishing when we got there. A well endowed female was doing a dance du ventre attired in a costume suitable to the climate. There was no entrance charge but the price of drinks was prohibitive – two lemonades, one beer and one whisky were $2.25. We had a dance there and then wondered from one nightclub to another until we got to the Florida at 1.30 am, just in time for the evening cabaret. This was an authentic one though the gestures in the Spanish songs were somewhat suggestive. As usual the beer was American and poor to my taste. We got back to the ship about 3 a.m. and though we could say we saw the nightlife of Panama we couldn't say that we were impressed. I had seen better at the Windmill in London!

At midday we left for Curacao where we stayed only long enough for me to buy a bottle of their eponymous liqueur!

The next port was Las Palmas and we were there only for a few hours. Unlike the outward voyage there was not so much fun. Everyone was short of money so my private patient income was very meagre.

Arriving in Liverpool was, for me, the end of a voyage of a lifetime and had given me a glimpse of the Southern Hemisphere and particularly the North Island of New Zealand I felt that what was needed now was some knowledge of the New World and to that end I searched for a ship in American waters.

The VILLAR was that ship and in 1948 I joined her.

CHAPTER THREE
SS Villar

SS Villar.

The SS VILLAR story starts in 1948 when I had just finished my second voyage in the Merchant Navy. On the 6th of January I left London's Heathrow airport in a BOAC York four engined aircraft bound for Montevideo. I had been taken on as a ship's surgeon to a Lamport and Holt Victory ship that was sailing into Montevideo in the next few days. This voyage would take me up the eastern seaboard of the Americas.

I had been told that though this ship was small and flew the Panamanian flag, a doctor would save the company at least £200 a day if he could sign the medical pratique that confirmed that there was no infectious disease on board and therefore allow the ship to go ahead into the port. If this were done at each port the savings would easily pay for my salary.

It was the middle of winter and I was wearing my blue uniform so that I soon appreciated that this was not the sort of clothing appropriate for South America. In those days planes were named after stars and mine was called Star Gaze. The stewardesses were Star Girls. By an extraordinary coincidence the chief pilot Harry Lincoln Lee had been at my school in Stockport though a little older than me. Flying in those days was more uncertain than it is now and it was not unexpected to be told that we would have to land at Lisbon and stay the night there because of engine trouble.

Apparently the coolant in the Rolls Royce engines was not working efficiently. As it was the closed season for tourists when we got to the Estoril Palace - the best hotel in the Estoril suburb of Lisbon - not surprisingly we were the only guests. As a 24-year-old in the presence of the two Star Girls I could not complain particularly as my pilot was an Old Stopfordian.

Surprisingly there was a dance on that night together with a casino. We danced until 1 am. It was rather disturbing to be called at 6 am and since I did not see any reason to get up early on the basis of the need for the aircraft to have some repairs I had a leisurely breakfast at 8am. I was told later that because my uniform had not only two stripes on the forearm but a red line between, the staff of the hotel thought I was the captain of the plane and woke me earlier that the real captain!

After taking off late in the morning we arrived at Dakar at 7pm travelling down the coast of Africa and seeing miles upon miles of desert and very beautiful green sea. Due to the lack of automatic air pressure control in the cabin I suffered from pain in my ears when we landed at Dakar. Unfortunately this was quite troublesome and at one stage I contemplated suing BOAC since it could have been prevented if I had been given a sweet to suck on landing instead of letting me sleep all the way down.

There was a change of crew at Dakar and I said a reluctant farewell to my girl friends and schoolmate. There were now eight passengers. One was quite intriguing. He was a middle-aged man who had the appearance of being a retired army officer (which indeed he was). What was so interesting was that he had a brief case attached to his wrist by what looked like a handcuff. His job, he told me, was to deliver important messages from the Royal family to heads of state. The brief case never left his arm.

We went across the South Atlantic to Natal. During the time we were waiting at the airport to take off we were given a plate of baked beans, which must have given him some difficulty in eating. After this refuelling stop we travelled down the coast to Rio de Janeiro. Sadly though we stayed quite a long time at the airport due to some more engine trouble I was not able to go into the city but contented myself with having seen the Sugar Loaf Mountain and the famous statue and Cococabaña beach. We had to go to Buenos Aires before finally taking off for Montevideo. Landing in the dark at Buenos Aires was thrilling to see the city laid out with the streetlights in geometrical rows.

The journey had taken two days. I was met by the Lamport & Holt agent, and taken to Hotel Gran Colon where I immediately went to bed. The following day it was raining but after going to the L & H office in Cervato Colle and getting a loan of money I had a wander round the city. After the Far East it was pleasant to see grassy parks and modern buildings. The afternoon was spent in my room trying to learn Spanish since the heat outside wearing my blue uniform was too much. Meals were taken in the hotel and seemed to have a bias towards pasta dishes. An early night was followed by another look around the town.

I appreciated seeing the shops with goods that were scarce in ours at home. I met the son of the manager of the L & H office with whom I went to a local beach in the afternoon. In the evening we went to the Dorchester Club where he was a member. This was followed by other clubs and a casino. Clubs all the world over usually revolve round the bar and rarely impress. These were really just bars without much character. To bed at 5 am!

The following night after a tour of these clubs and meeting a num-

Docks in BA..

ber of residents and a passenger who was to join the ship and travel with us to Buenos Aires I felt I had had enough of Montevideo's nightlife.

I was finally taken to the ship the following morning. The SS Villar, was three years old, 7,000 tons and a Victory ship similar to those made during the war as part of Lend Lease. It had a single propeller driven by steam turbines capable of a speed of 17 knots - a little different from the open steam engines on the Antilochus with its 11 knots and the Arawa's 14 knots.

Here I met Captain Kimmings who heads a crew of 50 together with the Chief Officer - Metcalfe and the Chief Steward - Barlowe.

Our passenger to Buenos Aires was a Mr Nesbitt. We had four other passengers - a Russian, a Swiss and two Argentineans. I was not clear where Mr Nesbitt fitted in!

After the Antilochus the accommodation was palatial. Not only was there more room but also everywhere was clean and well maintained and typically American. I had not realised that with my arrival the ship had assumed a new designation. We would get privileges if I signed the medical pratique and the ship did the New York to B.A. trip in less than 20 days. This meant that only in exceptional circumstances would there be extra calls in Brazil. However I gathered that the Polish engineers were not able to guarantee this sort of schedule and told me that if they pushed the engines too much they would break down. I just hoped this would happen near Rio de Janeiro!

There was accommodation for five passengers and from Montevideo to B.A. we had four. There was a Russian passenger who could not speak English but only German and Spanish; a Swiss who spoke no Spanish but German and English; an Argentinean who spoke English, Spanish and German; and an English-born Argentinean who spoke English and Spanish. What fun at the lunch table when three languages were in use. The doc kept his nose in the soup!

Into the "roads, i.e the approach to the port, and about ten miles from B.A.. The next morning we had to wait until 12.30 to see the port doctor and for me to do my signing. Despite this we were told that we would have to wait until tomorrow evening before we could go alongside. A long talk with the Chief Engineer - a Pole - was revealing. He had been in the English, French and Russian Navies during the war. All his officers were Poles but the deck crew were South Americans.

The first afternoon was spent looking at the equipment in the "hospital". This was quite a large cabin with an operating table and a com-

Belgrana swimming pool in BA.

prehensive set of medical equipment. In the event we arrived at B.A. at 1 pm but because of red tape we were not able to go ashore until 4 pm. Even then we were not really alongside since we were tied by the stern and so we had to go ashore by doing a bit of clambering.

My first visit to the city the following day was educational. All the streets were wide and parallel so it was difficult to get lost. The main ones were Florida, Corrientes and Saumiento. Florida was the most impressive with the opulent shops full of expensive goods. There were no traffic lights but at each cross roads a policeman in a raised box directed traffic. He seemed to spend most of his time eyeing the girls and when he went into action it was with loud whistling and waving of arms.

The nightlife starts late in B.A. and when I went with the Chief Steward to a film at the massive Rex cinema we did not go in until well after 9 and came out at midnight. Neon lights were everywhere and all the big stores were open late at night with windows that had moving tableaux rising from the ground and changing every few minutes. Even at midnight there were crowds walking the streets. The film was "Fugitive" and I thought that it was very poor! As expected the weather was hot (about 90 F) though not humid.

I had a so-called surgery every morning and I would get a few minor injuries, usually as a result of a drunken fight. Indeed most of the medical work revolved around drink and quite a few worried about what they had done whilst under the influence! The cost of all goods was so high here that I decided that I would save my money for New York where I was told everything was cheaper. Thanks to the Captain I was given an introduction to a Mrs Benedict who would arrange for me to go to her suburban house in Belgrano. This involved getting a train from the Retiro Central station. She met me there and introduced me to her husband and three teenage children - two boys and a girl - and sundry animals.

This area of B.A. was very residential and sported a fine club to which I was taken after lunch. Here I played two sets of tennis and had a pleasant swim. This was much appreciated since the temperature was again over 90 F. It was after midnight when I got back to the ship which had moved nearer the city but still not alongside. Thanks to this introduction I was able to go again to the Belgrano club the following afternoon, having done my dhobie (washing of clothes) in the morning. It was quite obvious that I had no function whilst the ship was in port since the last thing any of the crew wanted to do was to see the 'doc'. It was now the time that I was initiated into the time warp of B.A. in which the evening starts at about 8 p.m. and finishes at any time up to 4 a.m.

This was somewhat different from what I had been used to either at home or even on my last voyage. The usual form was to go ashore about 8 pm and have a walk along one of the wide avenidas window gazing and fantasising about what we would buy if we had the money. It all looked like Bond Street! Then perhaps a beer or two in a bar. The beer was bottled and usually pretty weak and insipid to our European tastes. A cinema was often the next port of call though occasionally we would go to a dance hall. Here like in Hong Kong there were dance hostesses who charged for the dance. Since all the dances were South American - either rumbas, tangos or cha chas we had to improvise quite a bit. Inevitably we met up with a variety of Merchant Navy companions of every nationality, many of them being North American.

In this fascinating city austerity was unknown and the sun shone all the time. The word 'beefe' here indicated a small 3-inch diameter 1inch thick fillet steak of indescribable tenderness and succulence. The fact that the herds were originally Aberdeen Angus may be an indication of their merit. Rarely did one order anything but a 'baby beefe' and French fries. Once again I met up with a Chivers who claimed to be the only Chivers in South America. He happened to be the father in law of someone I met at the Belgrano club. Surprisingly we traced our ancestors back to coming from the Forest of Dean. Some clubs were not favoured because they were so expensive. Not only were the drinks exorbitant in price but also it was inevitable that one would be approached by a female who would come and sit at the table and ask for "champagne". This was of course a very poor fizzy wine that cost an arm and a leg!

There was usually a floorshow that might be a couple of dancers doing flamenco with much noise of castanets. Once seen was enough. I mentioned before that as a result of my flight I had a pain in the ear due to not neutralising the pressure in the cabin when descending at Dakar. Normally the air in the ear absorbs and the pain goes in a few days but mine persisted. As a result I went to the British Hospital in B.A. and saw an E.N.T. specialist. I had in the back of my mind that I could claim off B.S.A.A, the airline, for this injury but I was told that my ear was quite normal and that the trauma would clear up in a few more days. Most disappointing! However I was shown round this seven year old hospital with its 300 beds. Not only was it beautifully clean and tidy but also airy.

I had a bit of luck that day as I got back to the ship just about noon. About ten minutes later one of the South American deck hands working on the bridge died suddenly. Fortunately I was there and though I could do nothing I got a Brownie point for being around and able to give a report. It was worth commenting on the fact that the Argentine at this time was very militaristic and much under the control of President Peron. There was a feeling of oppression everywhere and since I was able to satisfy the authorities of the cause of death of this man I, by so doing, avoided the company some red tape and waste of time.

I had examined all the crew when I joined the ship and had the medical history to hand. The Old Man, Chief Officer, Chief Engineer and I dressed up in our "No 10s", i.e. formal uniform, to go to the mortuary to identify the deck hand since it was not unknown for

Shipping congestion BA.

there to be a switch of bodies! This part of the journey was by underground. B.A. had about five miles of underground set out in a similar pattern to the one in London. There was a 10 centevos (1 pence) charge that allows for any journey and no ticket was issued since you just put the coin in a turnstile. Outside the mortuary we got into a fine 12-cylinder Packard limousine to go to the cemetery, causing quite a lot of interest from bystanders who thought that we were American Navy since they had just arrived in port on a courtesy visit.

The flat campus of Argentina.

Trip up the River Tigre.

The estancia in Santa Fe.

A funeral of this deck hand at the enormous B.A. cemetery was, of course, Roman Catholic but unlike many that I had been to at home was not very protracted. What was remarkable in this cemetery was that it had the appearance of a small town due to the size and number of mausoleums. All the relatives would be accommodated in each and some would be like small houses.

Since I was quite large and having a tendency to clumsiness I caused chaos and consternation in a nightclub when I accidentally knocked a waiter who had a tray of full glasses and siphons of soda water. The resulting mess was much regretted of course but being a foreigner was an advantage and I was not chucked out!

My worry was that I was not doing any medicine and inevitably when I left the Merchant Navy I would have to go back to some type of clinical work. As a result I tried to educate myself by reading a massive medical book. The particular one that I had taken out with me was called French's Index of Diagnoses. It had over 1,000 pages and had an exhaustive list of symptoms arranged alphabetically. Each day I settled down to try to learn from this tome. It was a forlorn hope!

Bearing in mind that there were only four English crew members on board it was apparent that we would soon tire of each other's company. The Polish engineers however spoke quite good English and I got on well with the Chief Engineer who kept me entertained with stories of the war.

Nearby were Dutch, Panamanian, French and Polish ships but I never got to know any of their officers. Each day I spent a number of hours walking the streets of B.A. and was most impressed with the width of the avenidas – avenues- and the size of the plazas (squares). The city was laid out in the same way as New York with horizontal and vertical roads. It was therefore easy to find one's way. The wide avenidas had the big shops and cinemas that impressed so much.

On one occasion the Chief Officer and I went to the Ballinerio that was an area devoted to amusements in the widest sense of the word. Here cafes and parks were well laid out and close to the sea front. Being alongside in a port one got a very jaundiced view of a city, only seeing a quay. The way that ships connected with the quay could be quite bizarre. Often one found that there were two ships alongside that one had to walk over before getting ashore. Occasionally, as it happened in B.A., we were tied by the stern to another ship and so one had to walk along the other ship's deck and then across another ship before getting on the quay. This was not too difficult in daytime but if the hatch covers were removed there were hazards. At night-time though it was not easy particularly if one had had a good evening!

Some friends of the Benedicts were going to arrange for me to have a weekend at an estancia (that was a sort of ranch where they rear polo ponies), which was about a hundred miles south of B.A. I had also an invitation to the Anglo meat factory that was the biggest in the Argentine. Here cattle and sheep were turned into either carcase or canned meat. Finally I had been invited by a dentist friend to a trip on his motorboat on the River Tigre.

I had a small adventure one evening when I thought I would go for a walk with only one peso in my pocket. The intention was purely to have exercise but on one avenida I heard the sound of American music and since this was very unusual I went inside the bar to listen. Since I could have a coffee for a peso I was able to sit at a table and get into conversation with an American sailor. He had been a door-to-door salesman in Civvie Street but in the Navy had a most unusual job to do on his ship. This was to clean out the filters on the destroyer's condensers. Water was sucked in and as a result fish were mangled up inside the filter. He said the smell was so strong that he could only manage three minutes in the area at a time. Our conversation was curtailed by a car's horn blaring out in the road outside. The poor driver was unable to stop it and just walked away. The noise was so great that the band had to give up and the waiters went outside and managed to pull the right wire.

The following day I swam at the Belgrano club and there met a young man who was going back to the U K the following day on the Highland Monarch (Royal Mail) ship. He came from Huddersfield and had spent 3 months in B.A. in order to learn the language. I saw him off and went on the ship. It was a considerable surprise to see one of the Arawa (my previous ship) stewards in the lounge. He said he couldn't get off the Arawa quickly enough. Why this was so was not made clear.

The news was that we had little cargo to carry and we were going to New York in a few days. There had been talk in the local papers about the Argentinean/Anglo negotiations. What the negotiations were about I did not know but I knew that the politics here made it likely that the breakdown would come from this side. President Peron and his wife Evita had been much in the news as a result of their being entertained by the two American naval ships - the cruiser Albany and the destroyer George K McKenzie. The politics I knew here I would

The B.A. waterfront.

not have traded for a Labour government at home since this was a corrupt dictatorship.

Vigilantes (policemen) were notorious for demanding cigarettes if they were asked to do anything. As far as life on the ship was concerned it was very serene. I did a so-called "surgery" at 9.30 am and attended to any minor accidents that occurred during the day. The "old man" i.e. Captain came from Liverpool and thankfully had a good sense of humour. Unlike many captains he enjoyed a joke even if it were against him. He was a keen philatelist and was collecting Argentinean stamps of 50 to 60 years ago. One of his daughters was studying modern languages at Liverpool University.

The chief mate was also a good type and had been a year on the ship. He played the banjo when he was feeling low! I promised to sing for him. This was guaranteed to drive him to drink! The third Englishman was the chief steward, and he, like the other two had a good sense of humour. I guessed that in this sort of job where you were cooped up with so many foreigners it was imperative to keep your sense of humour. The latter had a particular person whom he was always joshing. He was a Brazilian and chief cook. However he had been anglicised. David, as everyone called him, was as black as an ace of spades but always had a smile on his face and despite his age (reckoned to be over 60) had a reputation as a bit of a lad with the girls. The Polish engineers were quiet and the Brazilian crew were all right but were not given much leeway. They were born lazy and I became exasperated by my attempts to get them to do things.

I was learning more facts about the ship. It was 7,400 tons gross. Gross I was given to understand meant space. Space was measured in cubic feet and 100 cubic feet equalled one ton. This space was derived from not only the holds but also tanks, engine room and all earning space on the ship. Nett tonnage was holds and tanks alone. The gross tonnage was the usual figure mentioned. The cargo carrying capacity was either in deadweight (11,000 tons for this ship) or in volume (40 cubic feet equals 1 ton). The latter can thus be worked out from not only the cubic capacity of the holds but the deadweight.

My experienced fellow seafarers told me that this ship was not very stable at sea. On the subject of Victory ships, since this was one, it was interesting to note that at least 700 of them were made by the Americans. Villar was built in February 1945 when it was called El Reno Victory and was number 600. It became SS Villar in 1947. It stayed with Lamport and Holt for only two years after which it was taken over by a Dutch company and then two more companies before being scrapped in Japan in 1970.

One day I walked along the Balneario, Spanish for "promenade". It was evening and I had no idea what it would be like. I had on my white long trousers, Aden shirt and Malay rubber sandals. Imagine my surprise when having only walked a hundred yards beyond the end of the docks I came across a magnificent carriageway. It was festooned with lights and had avenues of trees either side. There were big cafes with tango musicians playing in the open and amusement parks for children. All this within a couple of hundred yards of the ship and I didn't know anything of it. B.A, had the finest docks from the cleanliness point of view that I had ever seen since they were so unobtrusive.

My very brief shirt, bare feet and general scruffiness normally caused conventional Argentineans to look reproachfully at me when I walked about the town. It used to be illegal to walk about without a jacket on but even now one had to wear a jacket and tie if one went into a café or nightclub. I suppose my excuse was that my experience of docks was of dirt and the fact that the town was right on top of us was quite a culture shock.

At the Belgrano club I met three pilots who had just flown from Montevideo that morning. They said the newspapers were full of bad news. Two British South American Airways planes had been lost. All these pilots were ex-R.A.F. and had to keep their self-confidence despite hearing bad news. I went to a few clip joints with them but since they had been up since 5 am we all had an early night. Belgrano club tended to be the starting point of most of my jaunts and on one occasion I met up with the stepson of my namesake and went to a place called "Nidito" which was Spanish for "nest". It was a restaurant where English was spoken exclusively. As in all cafes and restaurants here there was continuous music all evening. Inevitably a cross section of foreigners frequents these places and we met up with an American and a Frenchman. As a result of these trips to cafes I had developed quite a circle of friends. One of the detractions of these cafes was the unrelenting tango music. It was therefore those cafes where a wider selection of music was played that I favoured.

A weekend started a carnival. This was a national holiday which used to be celebrated by processions and lots of fun but had died down in B.A. recently. Rio was quite lively then but most people in B.A. tended to go to the coast - Mara del Plata – for their carnival. Mara del Plata was opulent and had casinos and beaches with surf.

I was becoming aware of the differential between prices of goods in B.A. and New York and home. It seems that home still had the edge and then B.A. The important point however was the availability of so many luxury foods, particularly tinned goods.

One of the problems of cargo was that it might not be available for transport when we were ready for it. As a result we had to be moved away from our place alongside the quay and instant access to the town to alongside another ship some distance from the quay because some cargo was not ready to be loaded immediately. This was what was happening now and we had to get a rowing boat to take us ashore. In a few days there would be a call and we would go alongside for the last time and when we had the cargo on board we would set sail. The boatman only worked week days and then only until 11 p.m. so there were restrictions. It often was not worth the trouble to get changed to go ashore and consequently I was doing much studying. It would have been helpful if there were someone who could have tested me on my newly gained knowledge. Watching ships go by was a pleasant occupation and when the Andes (a very large P & O passenger ship) came in on its first port of call on its first voyage there were some celebrations. President Peron went aboard the liner and had a few drinks.

An American passenger, Earl Nissen.

Carnival had started and seemed rather like a weak university Rag day at home. The most appealing features of the procession were the beautifully dressed youngsters. All were dressed in traditional Spanish costumes.

With my friends, the Benedicts, I tried mate tea, a herbal drink that traditionally was drunk from a gourd with a type of metal straw. It tastes rather like China tea but has no astringent qualities. The next day we set sail for Santa Fe which was not far away on the River Plate. The cargo we were taking to New York was mainly meat hides and some fats from the Anglo works. Here we got 600 tons of Quebracho. This substance was obtained from the tree of that name. The word actually being a diminutive of a word that meant, "Which breaks the axe". It was used in the tanning of shoes. The important point for the shipping of this cargo was that if it got wet it stuck to the ship like iron

Bele, on the Amazon.

and pneumatic drills or even dynamite might be required to move it.

Seventeen of the Brazilians were leaving the ship here and were now in the process of making merry. They would be greeted by a mixed group of children and mothers on the quayside.

I had got to know an American passenger called Earl quite well. He came from the Chicago region and though not wealthy himself had a relative who owned an important business and who looked after him financially. We often went ashore together and when we got to the mouth of the Amazon and the port of Belem this is what we did there, despite the heavy rain and high humidity.

We were not impressed with the statues that needed repair and there was a general run down appearance together with poverty. The only place we visited was the museum. It was also a zoo and an arboretum. All the trees of that part of Brazil were in the park. In the zoo were all the sorts of animals that one would expect - lions, tigers, monkeys and the brilliantly coloured birds of the forest. In the museum were relics of the Indian tribes. Shrunken heads were particularly of interest plus stuffed animals, birds and insects. There was even a six-inch stuffed centipede.

A Lamport and Holt ship astern of us did the New York to the Amazon trip and also went 1000 miles up the Amazon to Manaos. The filthy weather continued but I was told that it was preferable to the hot moist season.

We had to wait overnight for the boat to come off to take the pilot ashore. When it did turn up at noon it was a different type of yacht from the one we had seen on the way up river. I also noticed a man lying on the deck apparently asleep and undisturbed by all the commotion of coming alongside. The Captain told me that the other yacht (both their powered launches had engine trouble) had capsized and the man on deck was one of the survivors. They had rescued some but not all of the crew. Sharks and vicious small fish called "piranhas" which attack in shoals abound in the river and can strip a body of all flesh in a matter of seconds, so the chances of survival were small indeed. Up the river when the natives wanted to cross they sent a cow in first, which was promptly eaten alive. Then whilst the fish were busy the natives got across.

At Belem we picked up 200 tons of Toka beans, Coco beans and "Tomba" roots. The latter had a peculiar property being used by the natives for killing fish. According to the Captain if this root was shaken in the water a certain type of fish would be killed and rise to the surface. It was used commercially in the making of "Flit" the insecticide. We also took on animal skins.

However we were by no means fully loaded although we were getting some more goods in Trinidad.

Tomorrow we would arrive in Port of Spain, Trinidad where we would go alongside for about 12 hours for fuel and cocoa (600 tons). I hoped to get around the island as I was told the flowers were beautiful. I never forgot my pay was $129 a month (£32.5.0) when I went ashore to buy gifts but in Belem I was not troubled on that account!

My first impressions of Trinidad were of a lovely emerald blue sea and sky and well-wooded hills. The rate of exchange was 4 dollars to the £1. The British have the Yanks beaten hands down for quality. You ought to hear the Polish Chief Engineer go into raptures about British engineering and he has had 30 years of German, French, Polish and English and now American engineering. The Union flag still flies high though a little tattered!

Trinidad was not much as far as the town was concerned. The climate was pleasant and the coca-cola at the Queen's Park View Hotel was cool on that hot day.

We rolled and pitched ourselves into the North Atlantic, the temperature suddenly dropping one night a matter of 15 degrees F. This was when we got out of the Gulf Stream.

Having finished my French's Index to Diagnoses I started taking an inventory of the medical supplies on the ship. This included 20,000 salt tablets and about two gallons of Black Draught! This horrible con-

New York skyline.

coction was so foul that when given to a malingerer he never came back!

My only relaxation was playing poker in the evenings. I now know 18 variations. Fog descended the night before we were due in New York. Visions of a collision with the Queen Mary and the hooter going off every two minutes kept us all awake.

Then on Sunday lunchtime through the mist appeared the Statue of Liberty and the famous Manhattan skyscrapers. They seemed disappointing in the mist and looked very grimy. No doubt the recent snow, which had left the streets in such a deplorable state, had also left its effect on the buildings. In a few moments however another skyscraper showed up and this was impressive as it towered above all others - the Empire State Building.

We berthed at Hoboken, which was across the river from Manhattan, a dirty place but from the point of view of getting into the city much easier than London. Sunday evening I went to the Capitol Hotel where Earl had had a room booked by L and H. This was the hotel where all L and H officers were kept while waiting for ships home. The journey to Manhattan was via the Lincoln Tunnel using an American bus. Fares cost 20 cents (one shilling) to go to 41st street from Hoboken, as there were tolls to be paid on all vehicles through the tunnel. The buses were single decker diesels with the engine at the rear with air brakes and hydraulic doors operated by the driver. The driver who was called an "operator" sat on the left almost caged in by bars and a machine that was like a big cash register.

One paid a quarter (25 cents) or the exact amount and he punched the levers. If one was unacquainted with these buses it was a little confusing as a small ticket then popped up from an obscure slot and he flicked the change at you. At the end of the journey one gave him back the ticket. There were no gears on these buses so he drove with his left hand and counted his money, made entries into a schedule card and operated the hydraulic doors with the other. All this plus fast driving in densest traffic. I gave the Yanks credit for wonderful driving, unlike the Argentinos.

The tunnel was similar to the Mersey Tunnel but was longer though the impressions of Manhattan after the years of dreary darkness during the war could be imagined. Buenos Aires looked like my local village at home on a Sunday compared with Broadway. The heat from the electric lamps could be felt on the street. Animated signs drew cartoons or gave the news. In the case of the advert for Camel cigarettes smoke came out of the mouth of the painted face on the sign. Noise of jute boxes blared all around and it was typically commercial America as I expected it, but never could visualise.

Nearly every bar had a television set and one, called Jack Dempsey's, had a three or four foot TV screen which was reputed to have the largest in the world. While I ate clam chowder soup, frankfurter and cherry cheesecake I saw the television broadcast of the Chicago - New York Ice Hockey match at Madison Square Garden only about three blocks away. Last night there was boxing there. One can often see them from the pavement (I should have said sidewalk!) For fun we walked into the Waldorf Astoria and had a look around. I think I'll stay at the Astor, it has more class!

We saw the '48 Chryslers in the huge Chrysler building. I was with Earl, the former passenger. What tinny things they seemed but how sensible some of their gadgets were. For example, the old British system of signals by means of the direction indicators was completely superseded by lights fore and aft and on the control board which flash about once a second, so that from the front you would see a light over the left bumper and left rear wheel when turning to the left. Also a red flickering light on the dashboard. Admittedly more gadgets mean more things to go wrong but the advantages were obvious.

The weather here had been miserable and just like Manchester ever since we saw the Statue of Liberty.

Earl had to see about his train for Chicago so we went to the Grand Central Station. Unlike any station that I had ever been in there was no smell or signs of trains. The mural of a New England Village was prominent above our heads and the various departments plus the massive Hotel Commodore made the building look like an internal city. Having seen Times Square and its Flat Iron Building. 42nd street and a few of the principal buildings we had had enough. Naturally I got off the bus too soon at Hoboken and had to walk about a mile more!

On the next day Earl and I went "downtown". This was the Southern end of Manhattan where Wall Street was and the skyline that I first saw when we came in. I went to try to cash a cheque at the Federal Reserve Bank of New York and at other banks but my efforts were useless. We had a lot of fun going into them since they were in skyscrapers. I had bought a "Palm Beach" suit in Cibu City but as it was not attractive enough for New York I was on the look-out for a replacement in a material known as "shark skin".

I was interested to see in the newsagents that the American Sunday Times had 80 pages and weighed about a couple of pounds. One night I went to a play "Born Yesterday" and paid $1 80c for a seat. It was the story of a millionaire whose dumb mistress, having been given money to educate herself finishes up buying him out. The underground, called "tubes" were dirty, old, misleading and relatively more expensive than London. I was pleased to note the "one up" for the old country amidst the modern equipment.

However I had been spending a lot. Every night this week and one matinee had been spent in seeing shows. You may think this was where the money went to, but you would be wrong. I went alone and always in the Gods (maximum price $2). On Monday I saw "Joy of the World" at the Plymouth Theatre (45th Street). It was an amusing skit on Hollywood. On Tuesday I saw "Harvey" at the 48th Street Theatre. James Stewart had just come back to play in this show which he starred in on Broadway in November 1944. It was terrific! The show revolves around the mythical "Harvey" - who was a six foot five inch white rabbit. It sounds crazy but it kept everyone in peals of laughter. I hoped it would go to England. Wednesday was a big day as I went around the Rockefeller Centre in the early afternoon and the N.C.B. studios later and then saw "Allegro" at the Majestic Theatre in the evening.

I sent home a booklet that tells about this little city within a city. It exceeds the bounds of one's imagination. The view of the city from the top of the centre was very good as it was a clear day. The ship, the Queen Mary, went out whilst I was at the top - quite a sight. Also unlike from the Empire State Building one could see Central Park.

I met a Swede up on the balcony and he said the view from the Empire State was not as good as from the Radio City Building. One could see the whole of the island of Manhattan and the airport over on Long Island from it.

Even the roof gardens and underground shops and "concourses" were visited. No shop may be built under a street, as this was the property of the Corporation. As the guide said "Many of the workers never get any sun as there was everything that they wanted down there except for a cemetery!

At the National Broadcasting Corporation studios there was a 600-seat theatre - the largest in the world - and the massive switchboard was operated by three men. I saw and heard a "Soap Opera" It was called "Just Plain Bill" and was sponsored by a liniment firm. We were behind a glass screen but heard everything via loudspeakers.

Then I saw the Television Studios and was personally televised. This was quite an ordeal as the heat of the overhead lamps was terrific. Normally the air was at 30 degrees F when it was blown into the television studio but it was heated up by the lights to over 70F. In this experimental theatre there was no air conditioning and so the temperature was much higher than that. The rest of the group were in another room where there were six monitors and were able to see me on stage.

Yesterday I went to the Hayden Planetarium on 81st Street. The whole firmament was described from the setting of the sun, to sunrise. It was done by a big machine set in the middle of a dome. The effects were very realistic. Earl Nisson told me that the Chicago planetarium was even bigger. He would say that wouldn't he?

Then I went to the Radio City Music Hall. Fortunately I only saw the last of a film called "I Remember Mama" - a film I didn't want to see anyway! But the size of the place! 6,200 people could sit in the auditorium. There were three balconies and a massive ground floor. The show I saw lasted about three quarters of an hour. There was a fifty-piece orchestra and the 36 famous Rockettes. The latter were a chorus of girls who were precision itself. There was a trick cycling act and some singing. There was real rain falling on the stage (none of the actors got wet though) and other unusual stage effects.

One of the acts was called "The New Look" The girls were dressed in black except for certain parts that would show up with ultra violet light. This was on a darkened stage and the various stages of clothing through the ages were represented apparently appearing in space. To see this alone justified the charge of 98 cents! I left to have my favourite dish - a frankfurter and fresh orange juice.

In the evening I went to some studios to hear two shows. The tickets were free and were obtained by the Lamport and Holt office. I would have had enough of entertainment by then! Last weekend I had one night exploring Broadway having a small beer in each of the important bars. I went to Lindy's (famous for the gangsters in Damon Runyon stories but known as Mindy's in them), the Metropole (old time entertainment on a small stage in the middle of the bar) Mc Guinness's bar (revolving cartoons around the centre of the bar whilst sitting facing them) Jack Dempsey's - saw Toscanini conducting the New York Philharmonic Orchestra at the Carnegie Hall on the TV screen, and the Harlem Night Club - the night life of New York. Saw the show there whilst having a beer at the bar. I was told that the show was the same as that at the Coco cabaña and the Latin Quarter. The acts go from one club to the next.

Then I went to the Three Deuces on 52nd Street to see the Tin Pan Alley district. I managed to tolerate it for about ten minutes before leaving. Hot jazz was not my favourite type of music. Roseland Dance Hall was the biggest in New York and it was there that I met a Canadian and two Brooklyn girls. We went to a place called "Samoa" on 52nd Street. Here we saw low comedy of the slapstick kind. For 3.50$ it was expensive. That night I decided I had seen enough New York shows!

The following day - Sunday - I went a walk in Central Park with the girl from Brooklyn. We saw the lake and the baseball fans practising on the grass. It was a lovely spring day and quite a number of people were carrying portable radios so that music could be heard everywhere. Pauline (that was the girl's name) took me over to Brooklyn to a tea dance at the Knights of Columbus building. Here I met a lot of her friends but lost her! However I met a couple of typical Brooklyn lads who took me to another dance hall. I got a feel for the tougher side of New York life from them. That was the last time I went to a dance hall. Again I put it down to experience but not one I want to repeat!

The next day we sailed for Boston, Massachusetts where we would stay about a day, then to Baltimore and Philadelphia (both short stays). We may load coal at Norfolk (on the Delaware River) if the coal embargo was lifted. This would be for delivery to Rosario in the River Plate.

From Norfolk we would come back to New York to finish loading. I would tell the manager of L & H's office here tomorrow that I would be getting off the ship in New York next trip (about July). The idea in my mind was as follows. I would save as much as I could on the next voyage and then by means of a visitor's visa from the American consul in B.A. I would be able to spend a month or so on a lightning tour of the States.

The ESSO people gave me a map of the US and I planned to go to Chicago to see Earl (the passenger on the Villar) again and maybe spend a weekend fishing with him in the Wisconsin lakes. Then it might be possible to get to Vancouver. It would be a great opportunity to see some more Chivers as I did in Singapore and B.A.! Anyway it would all depend on money and time and what L&H had to say re sending me home from New York. Whatever happened I should leave this ship in New York next trip. The opportunity would be a wonderful one and would never come again with the restriction of pleasure travel and the inevitability of my settling down.

The political situation was also a factor. All countries were in a bad state. Here they were about ready to start war with Russia! Anyway live for the day I say.

To lighten the boredom at sea I bought a portable cum mains radio that cost $55. It was a short and medium wave set and a good investment as I could sell it in B.A. if I get short of cash down there. Since we left New York just over a week ago we had been to Boston, Philadelphia, Baltimore and now we were at Chester, near Philadelphia. The inland route to Boston was quite interesting as we saw all of Manhattan Island and Brooklyn with its famous bridge. Traffic jams on the narrow winding streets were frequent here.

Streets had typical English names and there were no numbered avenues, unlike New York. We were there only two days but I did more shopping there than on the whole voyage before. A sharkskin suit, which I had mentioned before as desirable was bought for $55. It had a long drape jacket with wide lapels and a light blue colour. Funnily enough the Americans called it the "English drape"! It fitted well despite it being ready-made. A second buy was the new Shavemaster electric razor. I saw a demonstration at a big Boston store by the Sunbeam salesmen. It was so impressive that I bought one. I also bought shirts and a tie, the former being of the collar attached variety. Their price was quite low - $2.90. I rather liked the new spread Windsor collars, unknown in England.

I did not do much sight seeing in Boston, as most of the places of interest were 19th century buildings where early pioneers and politicians lived. The Boston Park was the only place I visited. We only had a few hours at Philadelphia so I didn't go ashore. Anyway it was snowing - shades of England! I locked myself in my cabin with my radio. That day I heard actor James Mason and wife broadcasting from New York prior to a Hollywood visit. It was amusing as they did a skit on the sponsoring of shows in America. They did it as an English programme and so put the sponsors to shame. It was a pity I could not hear the dozens of medium wave stations that broadcast in this area. My radio was working very well despite my all steel cabin. The ariel was attached to that of the ship, as also was the electric current. The name of the radio was Amstrad and it had six tubes (we would call them valves) and three wave bands. It was smaller than a portable but has the distinct advantage of being adaptable to mains or batteries. It was my best buy ever!

Going to Philadelphia we had fog and a heavy sea due to going into the Atlantic. We then went up the Delaware River and through the Delaware and Chesapeake canal into the intricate and massive Chesapeake Bay. We got there on Easter Monday and my one thought was to get to Washington - which I did without delay. It was a lovely spring day and the journey by train only lasted forty minutes so I was able to have most of the time sightseeing. First I went to the National Gallery of Art where there was an exhibition of the paintings from the Berlin museums that had been discovered in a mine by the American Forces. It was quite an experience to see so many important paintings gathered together in one place.

At 2pm I went on a tour of the city and environs. Washington was a very open city. By that I mean that unlike any city I had visited it had large areas of grass and gardens between its big buildings. This was very refreshing after the claustrophobic atmosphere of New York. The guide who stood at the front of the bus and talked into the microphone was a Virginian and addressed us as a group as "Friends" and individually as "Brother" or "Sister". The Arlington Cemetery with its 50 or 60,000 graves and that of the Unknown Soldier was impressive but not as much as the one in B.A. The Pentagon building which cost 86 million dollars and which employed 45,000 people during the war was the origin of the story of the office boy who got lost in there at the beginning of the war who came out as a Brigadier General at the end!

The houses of John L Lewis and Eisenhower, together with the dwellings of other notables, including the Trumans' White House were "rubber-necked".

The general impression of the city was of quiet efficiency. Lack of "honky tonks" and glaring commercialisation was very relaxing. The Japanese maples, azalias and magnolias were out and these gave a refreshing atmosphere. I saw every thing under ideal conditions and so I rated it the best city to date.

On returning to the ship I decided to see a show in Baltimore. As I had lost my interest in films (Yankee anyway) I went to the Gaiety Theatre. This was a music hall that had burlesque acts. I thoroughly enjoyed it although I would tire of it quite quickly. The jokes would not get past the Lord Chamberlain nor would the stripper's dresses that had to be measured by the millimetre!

We had loaded 2,500 tons of coal for Rosario at Baltimore instead of Norfolk and were now loading general cargo for B.A. and Montevideo. This completed we left Baltimore and sailed south.

Life would have been monotonous if we had been long times at sea as I had no one of my age and nationality to talk to, but my interest in unusual places got me through OK. Also as I had many friends in B.A. the time there would pass quickly.

The Russian scare was hitting all the headlines and never a day passed without having more men needed for the American forces. Bing Crosby last night said, "A powerful America means a peaceful America". I had been listening to ABC (American Broadcasting Company) and the show, which debunked the sponsoring of various products, was the funniest on the American radio. It was called the Henry Morgan show.

Next day we sailed for Trinidad, Montevideo and B.A.. On the way we visited Bahia de todas los Santos.. The city was in two halves, an upper and a lower, the upper half being reached by lifts or a very steep road. The agent arranged for us to go to a "do" at the British Club that evening. We first went to the agent's house by means of a taxi that took us up the steep road through the city. We, that was the Captain, Chief Engineer and myself, met a number of members of a Royal Mail ship that was in at the time. We all went to the British Club where there was an elaborate buffet, which took a great deal of my attention off the sparkling conversation! A dance with an abundance of fox trots followed. Later a number of the members of the club put on a cabaret in which was our agent! The word "our" was used since it was revealed that he knew of me through contacts I had in BA. It was a very happy

Bahia.

occasion and even the Chief, who normally did not have fun, seemed to enjoy himself.

We were at Bahia for two more days during which time I only went ashore once more. This was at the request of the Captain who wanted me to testify that the ship had really encountered bad weather.

There were 365 churches in Bahia but I was wrong in thinking that this applied to the city. It applied to the State. The city only had a paltry 70. I told the authorities that the ship had had her funnel under water and that I had been inundated with work as a result of the fearful weather. It was not revealed to me what value this testimony had but assumed that it might have related to damage to the cargo.

The agent showed me the wonderful San Francesco church. This had all its carvings covered in gold leaf and was truly the most impressive interior I had ever seen. Coming back we descended via the lifts to the docks. At nighttime the skyline of the upper city was just like the back of a stage especially when the moon was up. Our evenings were spent on the topmost deck listening to the portable radio and looking at the stars. From leaving Bahia to arriving at Montevideo only took five days. The ship was beating her previous records and leaving all other ships at the post. It was strange that my ships were gradually getting faster and faster! The first 10, the second 14, the third 17 knots and coming home on a Cunard would be over 20.

Thanks to the two passengers life had been very pleasant recently. Conversation with them was in marked contrast to the sparse chats I had with the Captain and the Chief. Conversation with them was restricted to ten minutes at each mealtime. My experience with Captains was that if the conversation lasted longer than ten minutes it was possible that there would be an argument and all Captains were the same in being dogmatic. I gained the impression that anyone over 50 suffered from this complaint! I felt that the Captain should be called OXO since he was so full of bull!

The health of the crew was better but there was plenty of VD as one expects on this coast. I was getting very good at "short arm" bandaging!

The Captain remarked the other day that we must have had a Jonah on board as we had had such bad luck since leaving New York this time. By this he meant that we had had a lot of buffeting on the way down. The ship particularly felt this when it was lightly loaded - as we were now. The result was that we had to reduce revs because the propeller was out of the water so much of the time. The poor chief engineer who had been overworking and who was just recovering from an attack of kidney trouble worried himself into a worse state at the thought of his beloved engines being damaged.

So to Trinidad which was, on this occasion only remarkable for me in that I caught a 2lb fish, inedible of course !

Montevideo was only a short stay - a day - before we got back to BA. Here we lost our two female passengers who had been such good company on the voyage. It always struck me that this city was almost obscene in its luxury when compared with places like Bahia. There were the usual gentle pursuits that we had indulged in before.

Earlier I explained of my intention to have a took at the States before settling down into a life of doubtful obscurity. Negotiations were taking place between the American Embassy and myself and I was hoping to get a visitor visa shortly. We spent two weeks in Buenos Aires. The highlights were mainly evenings spent with the Sibbald family who had been extremely kind in inviting me round to their house for dinner on two or three occasions. One evening Dr Sibbald had a Jew - a Doctor Poppa at his house as the latter was over in the Argentine to give a demonstration of a new surgical operation. The family and Poppa and I went to a play in Spanish. Fortunately it was a musical that had such an unimportant plot that the defects in my Spanish did not spoil the enjoyment of it. I was not very impressed, with the standard of the beauties nor was Poppa. His remark on seeing the chorus was worth recording. He said "Were these the famous Argentine "beefes" I had heard so much about?"

Except for a very pleasant Saturday afternoon on the River Tigre I had not been to anywhere of any interest. My radio had been doing overtime. My pipe (I had not bought another) too was a very close friend and was so much a part of me that I was told to wear it when I had my photo taken, as I looked naked without it.

Once again we were on the move and this time only a short trip South. Leaving BA we experienced a roll and pitch due to the heavy swell and lack of cargo. For the first time I felt sick. However it did not last long and soon we arrived at another Bahia this time Bahia Blanca. Like the majority of Brazilian coastal towns it was a collection of small buildings and perhaps its only claim to fame was that where we were berthed the place was called Engineero White, presumably because of someone from the UK who had done something of importance there. The ridiculous thing about this visit was that we had come here for a mere 300 tons of wool. The freight on this would just about pay for the oil on this trip. We used 50 tons of oil a day at a cost of £8 a ton !

The unattractiveness of the look of the town meant that I stayed on the ship and saved some money !

So quickly back to B.A. for a week. before setting sail for New York. During this week and our final loading of cargo I paid the promised visit to the factory which supplied much of our cargo - the Anglo Meat Products. Here both sheep and cows were converted into a variety of mutton or beef products. In the foyer of the factory I was directed first of all into the waiting room for the factory dentist since this was quite remarkable. The whole of the inside wall was double skinned with glass so that fish could be seen gliding up and down. This aquarium would be very effective as a relaxant prior to meeting the dentist. The operation associated with the meat products was not so pleasant and somewhat cruel. The cows were prodded to walk up a long slope that led to the top of the building but the sheep had what was called a Judas sheep because it led the batch up the slope and when they got to the top it turned tail and ran back to the bottom. The fact that it was the only black sheep was its only protection. Once having gone through a door on the top stage the sheep were stunned with an electric probe. A hefty sledge hammer was used for the cows. The carcasses were hung by their back legs and their throats cut. From then on there was cutting of the carcase to eviscerate the abdominal contents and dismember the limbs. Suffice it to say these operations would convert any potential vegetarian. Having got to the very small portions there was the canning department. I used the word cruel for the operation but in fairness the cruelty would be mental stress on the animals and there was very little pain involved.

After a brief stop in Montevideo we set off for Santos. This was a first visit and its attraction was not helped by us having to wait a day for the pilot to come off. The appearance of the town was quite impressive and picturesque nestling as it did between hills. I went ashore with some officers to see a Bob Hope film. We picked up 300 tons of coffee as you might expect.

Since I was getting more and more unfit with so much to eat and so little exercise I decided to help the deck hands by ridding the fore deck of rust by using of a 24lb sledge-hammer. The Noel Coward line "Mad dogs and Englishmen go out in the midday sun" comes readily to mind. In addition when this was done I went round painting with red lead paint. I think it was a last fling knowing that very soon I was to leave the ship for ever.

Another visit to the mouth of the Amazon at Belem was uneventful and swift. We were glad to get away from the high temperature and humidity.

Then to Trinidad where this time I went ashore to an attractive arboretum where there were many exotic tropical trees including Flame of the Forest and Balsam of Peru.

Next stop New York. We sailed under the Verrazzano Bridge, named after the first European to see New York in 1524. The bridge seems to frame the wonderful sky scrapers of Manhattan Island. Forty two years later, together with over 20 000 other runners I would stand on this bridge at the start of the New York Marathon. The first event on arrival in New York was getting mail

I got two British Medical Journals (BMJs) the other day that were sent from home. The latest date was the 24th of April. This was how I heard of the BMA's decision to recommend to the Medical Profession to accept the NHS. I was rather surprised in view of a majority vote against it. There would be a definite reaction I was sure from that majority. Out here the reaction was that the Argentine would get a National Heath Service by the end of the year as it had come in England. It would be interesting to know how many doctors were trying to get out to the Colonies. The steel industry was next on the list I fear. Apparently there was some strong feeling against it as private enterprise was doing so well and the National Coal Board had been considered a flop.

I wrote to Norman Chivers, my second cousin who was studying psychiatry in Cincinatti, to warn him of my probable arrival in early July. I had noted the Cunard ship "Media" as a possibility for the return to the UK.

I got a ticket to Chicago from the Greyhound depot in 34th Street and went to the YMCA to look around, since I might be using it on my way back. It had 1200 beds, a dance hall and 8 billiard tables.

I then went to Harlem 133 Street 7th Avenue to a place called "Smalls" to see a show and then on to a dance at the Savoy on 140th St. This was famous for its jitterbugging. The next day I saw "Annie Get Your Gun" at the Imperial Theatre. Ethel Merman was impressive.

On July 1st with $340 I was able to leave SS Villar and set off at 11.35am on the Greyhound bus. The bus was comfortable but the air conditioning was not working. It went through the Pennsylvania Turnpike that had seven tunnels through the mountain. The stops on the route were only for 15 minutes and so just long enough for a quick call of nature.

A notice on the road caught my eye – "We don't know how to split the atom but for your whiskers just let us at 'em!". This was an advert for Burma Shave. A G. I. who was taking caskets (coffins) to families of the World War II dead entertained me with the story of his life.

I slept on the bus until 6am I noted a pleasant village called Warsaw. It took one hour to get to the centre of Chicago from the outskirts since it was 37 miles across. The Stephens Hotel with its 3,400 beds was considered the largest in the world, but I stayed the night with a friend of one of the passengers who came up to New York aboard the Villar.

A swim at the Montrose beach was followed by a visit to Michigan Boulevard and Grand Park. Whilst in Chicago I had seen an advert in a local newspaper for three people to join a car to drive across to Spokane. I contacted a man called Payne and arranged to meet him to discuss the trip. So together with two MIT teachers called Arthur Selfridge and Walter Pitts we drove off in this car which I did not notice, at the time, as being particularly memorable. We took it in turns to drive and this first day covered 770 miles driving non-stop.

The scenery was of large areas of farming land and open country. We were always well looked after when we filled up with "gas" by an attendant who checked our oil and cleaned the windscreen. The speed was constantly about 60 miles an hour since there was so little traffic on the roads. Occasionally there would be a sign at the side of the road "THINK" which would be the site of a fatal accident.

We stayed the night in a one eyed town of about 2,000 inhabitants called Chamberlain.

The next day we went through rolling hills with fields of sunflow-

Mr Payne with 1947 Ford V8

ers and then entered the Badlands, where there were the famous pinnacles of stone, some red some yellow. These were dramatic since they stood out above the flat surrounding land.

A feature of the roads in the wilds was the way that future towns would advertise by hoardings on the roadside miles ahead. Sometimes these adverts were for drug stores in a town and a specific product. One that was particularly appealing was – "Through this vale" - "Of toil and sin" – " The head goes bald" – "But never the chin" – "Buy Shavallo" There would then be the name of the drug store and the town a number of miles ahead. The notices would be a mile apart.

The famous monument of the four Presidents at Mount Rushmore was visited. Nearby we noticed an hotel called "Horse Thief" which advertised itself as a second-class hotel with inferior food!

At Cody in Wyoming we saw something that could have come out of a silent film. An old fashioned fire engine with firemen standing on the sides and bell clanging hit a car at an intersection. Neither were going fast but the result was quite hilarious with firemen flying in all directions.

We paid $3 to get into Yellowstone National Park and did the usual tourist visits to the colourful mud lakes and to see Old Faithful, the geyser, in action. We stayed the night in a cabin 20 miles away ($1.50 each).

Butte, Montana was our next stop. Here we learned of the most valuable hill in the world. This was where the smelting company Anaconda got its raw material – a mixture of silver, copper and tin.

Cody, Wyoming - a smash with fire-engine and car.

The tremendously high chimney of the works dominates the countryside for many miles. The scenery was obviously not very attractive near the town but a few miles outside was a lovely lake – called Georgetown.

This part of the country was on the Continental Divide and therefore rivers can flow either East or West.

Reaching Spokane at 9.30pm I said farewell to Mr Payne the owner of the car. Although a pleasant enough character he had an irritating habit of whistling through his teeth – out of key!

Now I had to hitch hike and so got on to route 10 and was fortunate enough to be picked up by a journalist student called Bud Higgins. He was driving a 1930 Model A Ford and had come from Rhode Island

Anaconda Smelting Works.

with the intention of going to Los Angeles. I drove the car for 20 miles and made the engine boil. We had to push it to a petrol station. The countryside was dramatic with mountains and giant fir forests. Since the car bonnet was loose and kept flapping we took it off. Passing Washington Lake we headed into Seattle via the Ponteen Bridge and tunnel. The YMCA took me in for 75 cents a night and I was alone in a long dormitory.

Bud Higgins and Model A Ford.

Through my Chicago friend I was put in contact with a family called Carpenter in Everett, a short Greyhound drive from Seattle. The father of the family took me to a local sawmill that dealt with giant cedar, fir and pine. Mainly it was used for housing. I tried water skiing on Lake Stephine but gave up because of banging of one ski against the other leg causing so much pain. Expressions used by the young here are "I know it", "Wasn't it though", "Go on a piece", "On the ball".

The following day I crossed the border into Canada and noticed that the houses and adverts were much more conservative.

Arriving in Vancouver I got a streetcar to E6 Avenue where Mr and

Water ski-ing at Lake Stephine.

Scenic tour of Vancouver.

Mrs John Chivers lived in a small bungalow. Their daughter Mary, husband Don Macpherson with their two daughters were there when I arrived. John Chivers was my father's uncle. He took me to Stanley Park to see the grizzly and other bears. Later I visited Vancouver General Hospital and learned about internships since I felt a genuine interest in staying in this part of the world.

The most exciting event of the stay was a rubber-neck tour of Vancouver in an open decked coach with Uncle John. The tour was well organized with surprising touches. At one stop a lady leaned out of a window and sang a short song. At another we all looked up and there was a blackbird on the top of a post that gave a chirrup. We were all asked to look to the top of a building where there was a photographer who took a photo, which we were given, at the end of the tour.

The next day I took a ferry across to Nanaimo on Vancouver Island from where I hitch hiked and with the aid of two cars got to Victoria. Here I met up with Canadian friends, Ian and Joan Williams. He served in the Canadian Navy in the war. They owned a 25-foot sailing boat berthed in Victoria. In it I sailed with them to Cork Bay, Ten Mile Point and the Uplands. Everywhere I looked there was evidence of the

Tour of the city in open top coach.

John Chivers (my father's uncle) and his wife.

most important industry in this part of the world – lumber.

There were many big logjams with watermen expertly balancing on logs using long poles with hooks on the end to manoeuvre them. I stayed with the Williams and the following day went on another cruise in their yacht aptly named "Con Brio". This time we went to Chatham Island, one of many small islands quite close to Victoria. Here we built a fire and cooked food and I slept under the stars in a sleeping bag. The night was warm and the stars were bright.

The next day I left Victoria on the Gulf Island ferry that lived up to its name. It called at the islands – James, North Pender, Morgue, Galiano, Salt Spring and finally going into Ganges Harbour.

Once again I stayed with the Chivers in Vancouver and went to a dance at the Pavilion in Stanley Park, the profit from which was going to provide food for Great Britain!

Starting my travels again the next day, I boarded a Greyhound bus for Portland, Oregon and then on to San Francisco. Noticeable on the side of the roads were signs where there had been accidents (S.O.S.) which meant Safe or Sorrow. Occasionally there would be the sound of a clanging bell indicating a locomotive passing alongside the road. Backs of lorries had up to eight red lights, which after our black out at home, was a bit of a shock. Since this was a long journey I slept on the bus.

It had been my intention to travel on the coastal road since this went through the Sequoias, the tall redwoods that I had read about. Unfortunately the Greyhound bus takes the inland route through Salim so I missed this treat.

Much sage bush and fires were seen in the dry hot countryside.

The Williams in pram dinghy.   *"Con Brio" yacht.*

Later fruit of various kinds were noted as I went over the Oaklands Way – 8 miles long. The lights of the Golden Gate Bridge and Alcatraz Island were very impressive. Alcatraz was still a prison.

No luck in getting into the YMCA, but I got in to the Balbroke Hotel off Garden Gate. It was quite central and only $1.60 a night! I saw a type of concrete mixer on a lorry that turned as it went along and kept the concrete from solidifying. I met a relative of my second cousin and was driven by car up Russian Hill, Nab Hill and Telegraph Hill. Here was the Coit Tower with interesting murals, though in itself a monstrosity. I went through Chinatown, but it was not to be compared with Singapore. On Fisherman's Wharf we had a seafood salad. It was very picturesque with the boats alongside the shore. Both lobsters and crabs were boiled outside in the streets. The highlight of the visit was to go to the "Top of the Mark" which was the cocktail bar in the Mark Hopkins Hotel. From there, there was a panoramic vista of S. F. including the lights of Alcatraz prison.

The following day I caught the bus to L A. The bus went via Fresno and Bakersfield. The heat and the lack of air conditioning meant that many drinks were drunk and ice creams eaten. I arrived in L.A. at 2pm and I went straight to a YMCA where I booked a dormitory bed. Impressions of this Central Valley were of an arid brown landscape with rows of trees and houses accompanied by the usual gaudy signs.

The following morning I rang my second cousin, Evelyn Drennan and visited her at West Chester, 15 miles outside the city. She had two daughters - Mary - 12 and Jane 8. I was taken by car on a tour of Hollywood and Beverley Hills and saw Grauman's Chinese and Egyptian theatre where the hand and food prints were shown in the concrete entrance. These were of famous stars. On a 30-mile drive out of the city many big houses were seen most of them were too close together. L A was over 30 miles long. However the area of L A was 45 square miles and there were 3.5 million inhabitants and 1 million vehicles.

In Hollywood there was no sign of the movie industry. Traffic was fast and dangerous. To cross the road one had to get to an intersection and wait for a wooden board to go up with the words " Walk now " on it. At other times there was a board with the words "Don't walk".

The important event of the next day was a visit to the Hollywood Bowl. This was set in picturesque surroundings in a valley. Two blue searchlights were pointing straight up. I was told that this was to discourage aircraft. The amphitheatre was large and we were at least 250 yards from the stage. Jose Iturbi and his wife Amparo were the prime artists with a symphony orchestra, which played Tchaikowsky and Liszt. It took an hour and a half to get there by public transport in two buses and two hours to get back.

The United Artists theatre, which was a cinema, was visited the following day and Abbot and Costello in "Frankenstein" was the film.

One of the tasks I had set myself was to look up the daughter of the landlord of my local pub in Disley. She had married a GI during the war and had gone back to America with him. I found her with her three and a half year old daughter in a rather shabby apartment. She told me she was divorced and was not at all well off. I brought her up to date with local news and felt sad for her.

I went to the Santa Monica beach where I was hoping to see the great rollers. Yes they were big, however I was disappointed in the distance that they went up the beach. At Wooolacombe in Devon though smaller the waves went further. That evening I went to an old-time Music Hall where there were tables laid out and beer was drunk. The audience were encouraged to boo at appropriate times. It was great fun. Once again I missed the last bus and had to hitch hike back to the Dennnans' home.

It was interesting the next day to visit Olvera Street in Hollywood since this was the Mexican quarter and the oldest part of L A. In contrast to this very colourful and ethnically correct area was the poor quality of the Chinese quarter. Whilst in the Mexican quarter I was introduced to Tequila. This was Mexican gin taken with lemon juice and a thin layer of salt round the rim of the glass. Quite a distinctive taste. Finally that day I went to a Hawaiian nightclub that had exotic music.

At this point in my travels I tried to summarize my thoughts on this part of the country. The most impressive thing about L A was the distances between the suburbs and the town centre. And there were so many cars. The bright blue sky and lovely climate with only the white trails of the planes writing out adverts in the sky. This contrasted with the urban sprawl of car selling lots, electric pylons, oil rigs and advertising signs together with the complete lack of any planning of the houses. This ugliness contrasted with the immense vitality of all the inhabitants, all of whom seemed to be working at break neck speed.

Pasadena and lovely houses led on to the Huntingdon Library after lunch at Van den Kapps restaurant. The library was in a large estate with flower gardens. Rembrandt's "Blue Boy " and "Pink Girl" were the great attractions. Melody Inn and Lindy's and finally the Bar of Music completed my education of Hollywood.

I met Max Marshall, the owner of the car in which I was to drive to Chicago in three days time who seemed a pleasant type. He had a 1940 Ford Convertible. I arranged to give him $30 for the ride. As we left L A I was disappointed with the closeness of houses and industry and particularly the oil derricks. Town planning was not in existence here.

David Brunskin was the other driver. We drove through Pasadena and through the Mojave Desert on the State Highway. The weather was very hot and as a result the engine boiled many times. Sand, cacti and mountains were the main features of the countryside.

We arrived at Las Vegas at 5pm but drove on to Boulder City where we saw films of the construction of the dam. We went into and down the inside of the dam by means of a lift. We drove back to Las Vegas and saw the gambling using silver dollars. We soon left and drove

1940 Ford V8 convertible.

Mojave Desert, Nevada

through the night. During our conversation I discovered that David was a Jew and Max was of Romanian stock.

At first the land was arid but then became more green as we went along. Iron ore was found round here. We arrived at Salt Lake City and went to see the Mormon Temple and the Capital. We drove on through more hot and sparse countryside and noted that the earth was coloured in shades of red. However there were now wooded mountains, the Rockies, which reached 5,800 feet up. We stayed at a place called Maybell on Route 40 at the Victory Hotel ($1.80 each) where we noticed that both the windscreen and one of the front lamp glasses had been broken by flying stones.

We left for Denver at 9am via the Rocky Mountain Park that went up to 12,000 feet. We saw chipmunks and wild deer. We past through Roosevelt Park and drove through the night, via Colorado into Nebraska and on for 200 miles and then slept until 7am. Most of the time we were keeping up 55 miles per hour.

We arrived in Lincoln, Nebraska and then went on to Omaha and Des Moines. Corn on the cob seemed to be growing everywhere on the flat and wooded landscape. We had trouble with the dynamo and had to buy a new one. I was starting to get a little irritated by David's conversation, which seemed to focus on people's dishonesty.

We had fun with the sack of Californian oranges we had brought with us. Since this was an open car we threw oranges to any pedestrians who seemed friendly. I had a frightening experience whilst driving through the night whilst the other two were asleep. I was driving alongside, but unseen by me, a railway. I saw a light approaching on my right side and thought it was a car on the wrong side of the road! The train with its bright headlight went by with a great roar and frightened the life out of me. Max had been a pilot and had made the steering wheel of the car into the shape of the joystick of a plane. It was butterfly shaped and so had no top or bottom! This made turning somewhat hazardous if undertaken in a hurry.

We arrived in Chicago at 7am and rang the friend of the passenger whom I had befriended on the Villar but gathered that life was a little complicated since he had become estranged from his wife. So we drove on to Akron in Ohio sleeping in the car, as we could not get into a YMCA there. This was the third night in succession we had slept in the car and we had travelled 3,000 miles in less than five days.

The farms were scattered across undulating countryside growing apples, cereals and potatoes. Max had a sister in the vicinity and we had breakfast with her. He had seven sisters and brothers in Pennsylvania and Ohio. I walked around Akron, which was the centre for the rubber industry. I met Max's brother Lyn who not only built his house but also his trailer and scooter. He had a daughter who was an epileptic and had adopted a boy of four. Lyn had had a gas station but it was burned down a few months ago and now he was rebuilding it.

Refreshing rain came down which allowed me to watch Lyn make window frames. We left after lunch for Ebensburg, which was 75 miles East of Pittsburgh. Here we met another of Max's brothers called Wils, whose house was built by Lyn. Lyn seems to be the only member of the family that had any ambition and that was to be a lecturer in maths and economics.

This was where I left Max with his family. I now hitch hiked – two lifts to get to Pittsburgh and then ten more to get to Lafayette on Route 22. The characters I met included a preacher, a dairyman, a whiskey salesman, a labourer, a furniture maker, and a student. Some of them had been in the war and served in England. One proudly showed a hand that had lost four of its fingers as a result of a bombing raid on Southampton.

I stayed the night in a truck driver's dormitory (25 cents), as there was no point in hitch hiking at night-time. There had been a murder near here on the road that had involved a hitchhiker.

On the road again at 7am but it was three quarters of an hour before I got a lift and then only three miles to London, Ohio. The next driver was going to Florida. We stopped at the Wilberforce College for

Author with chipmunk.

Negroes and then six more hitches before I got to Cincinnati.

I had had 36 lifts to get there! Mostly from labourers.

I waited for my cousin, Norman Chivers at the hospital. He was doing a psychiatric course there. He took me to see the Chicago Cubs beat Cincinnati Reds at baseball. Then to a nightclub called the "Cat and the Feather" where we were entertained by strippers! We were encouraged to show our appreciation by hitting the tabletop with miniature hammers.

Norman had bought a 1940 Oldsmobile the day before and I was allowed to drive it to St Charles Place where I met Shirley Dittz who was the secretary to the Psychiatric Department. I drove across the Mason/Dixon line into Kentucky and enjoyed relaxing in the sun.

I went to "Doc's Place" for Southern Fried Chicken ($2) then to an open-air drive - in cinema in Dixie Gardens. A loudspeaker was attached to the door of the car. Though left hand drive and hydromatic (i.e. no clutch but use the gear lever) it was easy to drive.

After lunch I went to Shirley Dittz's home and drove out to Harran in Indiana and walked by the river. We had a Bar B Q of pork ribs at a place called the Hickory. Later we saw a film - "Canon City". Shirley developed an irritation of her legs, which may have been due to poison ivy. This caused some ribald comments from Norman and his friends. The next day I met some of the 100 residents in hospital and had an interesting morning walking round the local zoo and seeing the mess that had accrued from the weekend litter louts. I was disappointed in the condition of the animals.

Later I looked in a second hand car sales place for bits for Norman's car and I spoke to the Lamport and Holt office in New York and heard that I was booked on the Parthia to go home. I then went to Norman's girl friend's home in the evening with Ed, Polly Beard, and Kay Latter (Ed's girl friend) where we were dancing and drinking in the "Rumpus Room". I tried unsuccessfully to jitterbug.

At 3.15pm I left by bus for New York, via Pittsburgh where I changed buses. I slept well and arrived in New York at 2.30pm on the 28th. I met a lad on the bus who had left New York for L A and when he got there had decided after two hours he did not like it and came back. He had been 12 days on the coach and had passed through 20 states.

After going to Hoboken, which was where my ship used to berth, I found a small hotel called the Pier View ($1.50 a night). The room was on the 3rd floor and had 2 skylights but was clean. When I went to the Lamport and Holt office the following day they told me that no money had come through from the U K and that I was to be given $20 for the voyage home and $5 a day subsistence allowance whilst in New York. As a result of this I walked everywhere and lived on hot dogs and frankfurters.

I bought some soap for home and with $19 left went on to the Parthia. This 13,000 ton Cunard ship was only four months old and had 250 first class passengers. The only notable event was that I played Bingo for the first time and won 30 shillings. I also met the ship's doctor who told me that he had had to perform an operation after the ship was only 17 hours out. He did the abdominal operation under local anaesthetic successfully.

On August 28th I arrived back in Liverpool. Many years later at an evening class I met Gordon Salisbury and discovered that he had joined the Villar as a chief officer a week after I had left. We often met to reminisce about life at sea.

This was the end of my Merchant Navy service except for a week spent on a new Alfred Holt ship called the Autolychus on which I was asked to act as surgeon when it went on trials. The two interesting aspects of this week were that we visited the remote island of Fair Isle and that on board was one of the descendents of the Holt line – a Mr Holt. Although a millionaire I was surprised that he wore a shiny old raincoat!

Within a few weeks my calling-up papers came for the Royal Navy...

CHAPTER FOUR
The Royal Navy

RN Medical course. The author is on the right at the back

I was called up to do my National Service in the Royal Navy in August 1949 without regard to the nearly two years I had served in the Merchant Navy. One might think that this was unfair but at the age of 27 and with no definite leaning toward any branch of medicine I looked upon it as more useful experience.

Originally National Service was for two years but by the time I went in it had become two and a half years.

This service could be divided into five parts. The first was the introductory square-bashing in Portsmouth, together with training courses. Then there was a spell of examining young entrants at Corsham, in Wiltshire, followed by another short period examining new recruits in Liverpool. The rest of my time was at Bramcote, near

Nuneaton. Finally I had a very short period at sea on an aircraft carrier and a mine layer. The latter, strictly speaking, was a bonus as part of my R.N.V.R. commitment.

The first month in Portsmouth was idyllic since my fiancée, Jean, was able to live in a hotel in Southsea whilst I was quartered in the Naval barracks. Although my uniform was, of course, strictly Royal Navy I kept my Merchant Navy hat and put the Royal Navy badge on it. Since the Merchant Navy hat was smaller it caused a certain rakish appearance and there were a number of "double takes" from the instructors!

We doctors and dentists were a small group and had to do the usual square bashing that the rest of the Navy did though being professional men it was expected that we would be no good at it. That was very soon evident! We each had to go in front of the group and order them about. Obviously there were the hilarious results of walking into a wall, or not being able to "fall in" properly, or some turning one way and some the other type manoeuvres.

Germ warfare was just being admitted as part of modern fighting and so there were lectures on the many diseases that we knew about anyway. Films featured quite frequently in these training sessions. Anti-gas training involved some practical sessions in which we wore gas masks and went through real gas (I suspect it was only tear gas!).

One of the more exciting courses was in the use of firearms. We learned how to fire a revolver at the Gunnery School on Whale Island.

At this time I was the owner of a 1938 Morris Minor 4-seater tourer that I had had for about three years. It was during this month that I saw an advert in a local motor magazine for the sale of a 1924 Humber Chummy open tourer car for £60. It had been owned previously by the Hon Harvey Bathurst and with a pedigree like that who could refuse. The Morris Minor went to a colleague on my course.

The Humber was fun! It had only one door and that led in to the nearside front where there was a bench seat with the passenger's backrest hinged to allow entry into the rear two bench seats. In accordance with its age it had no synchromesh on any gears and the gear lever was on the driver's right together with a hand brake that was connected to the rear wheels only. The foot brake was to the transmission and was a band that tightened round the propeller shaft going to the rear wheels. Neither of these methods produced startling results but since the car never went more than forty miles an hour there was little need for too much worry on this score.

1938 Morris 8 and 1926 Humber.

The gear lever moved into notches. In order to start, the clutch was pressed down and the gear lever put into the left top notch. However to change from first to second required skill. Firstly the foot was taken off the accelerator at the same time as depressing the clutch. The gear lever was brought into the centre of the gearbox and the clutch released and at the same time the right foot pressed on the accelerator. This was the tricky bit that only experience determined. When the engine was revving at the right speed the clutch was again depressed and the gear lever brought to the left lower notch.

All this was performed in a matter of seconds and if all went well the operation of moving the gear into the next slot was classically described as 'cutting through butter'! The novice would either not get into the gear at all having to listen to a nasty grinding noise or get in with only a token grind. It was worse changing down since then the revving between the gears was more critical. The clutch was a leather cone that engaged to metal and had about a quarter of an inch traverse. Considerable skill with movement of the left foot was required to get a smooth take off. In order to make the use of this clutch less dramatic an occasional drop or two of linseed oil through a little hole in the top of the gearbox was required.

A knowledge not only of old fashioned driving but the way that an internal combustion engine worked was required. Levers on the top of the steering wheel were for adjustment of the throttle and the ignition. The latter was particularly important since ignition could be advanced or retarded. If retarded the engine ran hot. More will be related on this phenomenon later. It was a Royal Blue colour and had a hood and side screens that had to be pushed into four slots. One could not say it was draught free! To be able to drive it without causing comment from either passengers or the bystanders required a certain amount of skill and to be able to double declutch (an expression unknown to the modern driver) and feel the gear lever move noiselessly into the next gear was an almost ecstatic moment. To make one's presence felt there was a Klaxon horn. Although electric it had a sound rather like a thousand crows in full cry!

The final problem was that there was no petrol gauge. In fact, the only instrument was a speedometer. The lack of a gauge meant that running out of petrol was not an infrequent hazard but a gallon of petrol was usually a smelly cargo in the back.

The Navy's working day was a short one with a 9 to noon morning and 2 to 5 afternoons. My duties were to look after the Receiving Room in the Barracks. This was like a Casualty Room in hospital but not as well organised. Everything that went wrong medically with any Naval personnel came in here and so most of the cases were trauma. It was not onerous.

The evenings, which were quite long since this was August and pleasant, were spent on the beach or in the theatre on the pier.

My colleagues were interesting. One had played Rugby for Oxford University and another, a dentist, was later the President of the Royal College of Dentistry. He put in a gold filling on a molar tooth that was commented on favourably by my civilian dentist when I came out of the Navy.

The month's induction was followed by a posting to HMS Royal Arthur. This was not unexpected since in my Merchant Navy account of my voyage on the Arawa, a Surgeon Captain Quinn had said that if I should have to do National Service (proper!) I should opt for the Navy, and mention his name since he was the Chief MO of Royal Arthur.

This was a shore-based establishment for the examination of new recruits to the Navy. Prince Philip had been there in the days when he was engaged to Princess Elizabeth and indeed there was a large portrait of him in the Officers' Mess. Situated near Corsham it could not be in a more beautiful part of England. Nearby was the lovely old village of Laycock and Bath was not far away.

The problem was that it was 250 miles from my fiancée and with

Popino (the name I gave to my car) having a maximum speed of forty miles an hour ten hours was about par for the journey.

I had a pleasant meeting with Surgeon Captain Quinn and soon settled into the routine. When one had to examine many fit young men who had already had an exam before getting into the Navy boredom soon set in. It was a source of wry amusement when a contemporary of mine who was a Surgeon Lieutenant at HMS Ganges, where our youngsters went after their examinations, complained that I had let in a bed wetter! He did not explain how I could have detected this at an examination. However bed-wetting was one of the sure ways of getting out of the Navy and maybe he had had enough when he had only been in a few weeks.

Other than examinations I had to give lectures on First Aid and Hygiene. In a First Aid class I had to deal with one lad who fainted when I was talking about VD. This subject was, of course, of great interest to all sea faring fraternity and they usually liked to know the details. I had one lad in the class whom I had been told was a narcoleptic. This meant that he went to sleep without warning. I had to seat him at the front of the class on a stool and with a long billiard cue prod him from time to time! He used to fall on parade and, of course, was soon invalided out. The medical examinations in those days had an acronym PULHEEMS. These stood for Physique, Upper limb, Lower limb, Hearing, Eyes, Ears, Mental condition, Skin. There was a routine, which involved others, who had to test urine and visual acuity but the hands on was done by the doctors. It was extremely difficult to be mentally sharp after examining more that six at a session.

For one week I was sent on an Atomic Warfare course to Portsmouth, which was a very welcome change. Here I learned about Geiger counters and how much radiation would kill a man. Since I had a school chum who had been in Nagasaki as a prisoner-of-war and, by virtue of being in a cellar when the bomb went off, had escaped with no radiation effects, I felt that the secret was to keep under ground as much as possible.

I had at that time a contemporary who, like me, had opted for M.N.Service and was now in the Army, staioned fairly near Corsham. He and I had been on leave and he came down with me in the Humber from Cheshire, leaving home at 10pm. We almost got to Corsham when the engine boiled as a result of too retarded ignition. Foolishly I loosened the cap on the radiator and a fountain of rusty water went about twenty feet in the air. Luckily I only had a slight scald on my hand but it was a frightening episode. We ran out of petrol just before the gates of Royal Arthur and had to be ignominiously pushed in! We arrived at 8 a.m. and I had to give a talk on stress at 10.15. It was quite easy since I could tell them what it was like to drive a 1924 car for 250 miles in the dark !

Having arrived in Royal Arthur in early September I was told that it was going to close down in November.

I was posted to the Liverpool office in early November to examine new recruits. For some reason the Admiralty realised that I could save them some money, as I would be able to live at home and travel to Liverpool by train and examine the relatively few recruits and get home the same day. This was even more pleasant than life in Portsmouth since I had two hours each way on the train from Disley, via Manchester, during which time I could read a book, Boswell's Life of Johnson.

The examination was a little different from the sort I had met in the Merchant Navy, or indeed Royal Arthur. I had to work out the vision using corrective lenses since the Navy was keen on both visual acuity and colour vision. A bizarre part of the examination was to look at the anal region. I was told that one could recognise a homosexual by the presence of a funnel anus! This was not something definitive and no one I saw showed this sign! I examined no more than six a morning which took about two hours. I was back home by tea-time.

Of course, this could not last very long. It was too good to be true and three months later I was posted to Plymouth Barracks. Here I had to perform the usual casualty functions and odd jobs including looking after the patients referred from the Detention Quarters. This Naval gaol was a tough place to be kept in. Usually naughty ratings were sent there for short periods for minor offences – drunkenness, absence without leave or other indiscretions not requiring a court martial. Here everything was done at the double and the inmates became very fit having to run everywhere. They had to stand to attention on the parade ground when smoking the allowance one cigarette per day. A Petty Officer then made them put their cigarette ends into an empty tin. My patients usually had had some accident such as falling on the face whilst deeply inhaling a cigarette or having a fight with another seaman.

It was not demanding work. The company was congenial and there was plenty of time off. After a few weeks I was sent to H M S Siskin to an Air Medical Course. It was ironic that at the beginning of the War when we all had to state our preferences for our National Service I had opted for the Fleet Air Arm as a pilot. In retrospect looking at the fate of Fleet Air Arm pilots in the war I was lucky I was not called up for that role.

Siskin was the Fleet Air Arm training centre and here I was given a two weeks' course in all medical aspects of the service. Films and lectures in aeronautics were followed by interesting practical demonstrations such as entering a decompression chamber to experience the effects of high altitude. The five of us were crammed into this tank with bench seats facing each other and waited. We were told that this time we would be going to 22,000 feet and to talk about our impressions. Euphoria was the obvious one. We all made facetious remarks and noted that our voices were pitched at a much higher level. The other cause for amusement was that due to the effect on the bowels the atmosphere became somewhat smelly.

The next practical outing was to the Naval baths where we were strapped into a mock cockpit and dropped twelve feet into the deep end of the baths. We had to unstrap ourselves from the harness and the parachute on our backs in order to get into an inflated dinghy. It was exciting but relatively easy and not as dangerous as it sounds.

We were subjected to the decompression chamber at a simulated altitude of 40,000 feet and this certainly made us feel ill. In fact one of our colleagues fainted. It had an effect on my ears that took some days to recover. I now know what the point of this extra height was other than to highlight that lack of oxygen could make you faint.

HMS Gamecock

As doctors we were given detailed instruction in how to examine aircrews. This was perhaps the most valuable part of the course. One of the ways of testing for lung fitness was to get the subject to blow into a sphygmomanometer. This instrument for measuring blood pressure has a cuff. When this is removed the tube, which is still connect-

Officers' Mess - Gamecock.

ed to the gauge, is given to the subject. He is asked to blow into it and keep the mercury level at 40 mm for two minutes. If he does he has passed the test.

There were some interesting tests for speed of reaction. One that was fun was to hold a ruler against the wall at about five feet from the ground and get the subject to sit down with his right hand ready to hit the ruler on its way down. Since there was no warning as to when this was to happen it was quite an instructive test. Again eyesight was an important aspect of the examination and we had instruction in testing for not only normal and peripheral visual acuity but also night vision.

Surprisingly enough the course even covered what to do if you landed in the jungle. Near the end we had to prepare a short talk. One wag gave us an amusing account of the effect on the love life of the tortoise on being subject to high altitude! My contribution was much more mundane as it was on the geological wonders of Rotorua. On the last afternoon we had an exam, which was not difficult.

For the next ten days until the end of March I was kept in the routine at the Barracks.

I was then posted to a Fleet Air Arm Station near Nuneaton called HMS Gamecock. It was there that I served the rest of my time in the Royal Navy. This was rather a contrast to the last two years at sea in the Merchant Navy. Lutyens designed this station. There were a number of buildings to accommodate ratings who were to be trained in aircraft maintenance. Schoolrooms, workshops and hangars were scattered over a large area and beyond them was an aerodrome. All the buildings were relatively new and in very good condition. There were even two squash courts, which were put in to help pilots to keep their eyes and reactions in trim – or so I was told.

Surgeon Captain Norsworthy was the Principal Medical Officer and I was his assistant. There was also a nursing sister, a Queen Alexander nurse and two dentists. All of the medical and dental staff were in the same building. Two, ten bed wards and a spacious surgery were very welcome and rated the best of all those I had met before!

Tiger Moths - On Fleet.

Work was not onerous. There were few hazards and the vast majority of the officers and men were young and fit. As usual I had a morning and evening surgery that only took a short time. From noon until 2pm was lunch-time and one of the dentists, John Brammer, and I played squash after a speedy lunch.

I had been married at the end of 1949 to Jean who was able to join me and live outside the station in Nuneaton. She lived in what was known as "digs" in those days. That meant that she lived with two other ladies, one the owner of the house and the other also a lodger. This semi-detached house was in a cul-de-sac close to the centre of Nuneaton and very close to a church. The latter was somewhat of a nuisance since bell ringers seemed to have a practice each evening! These two ladies were congenial and the lodger being a schoolteacher related to Jean, who had been teaching until recently.

Life was very pleasant. I played wing three-quarter for the station rugby team and went with them to play at neighbouring establishments – usually army. Minor clinical work was interspersed with lectures on hygiene or first aid and occasionally I had to do some vaccinations or pre employment exams.

Quite apart from the squash court there was a cinema and a large room used for dances. We even had a concert there to which the PMO's wife gave us a rendition of a few modern ballads.

Being an operating aerodrome there were occasional excitements when aircraft did odd things. One of our aircraft landed near Birmingham in a field because it ran out of petrol. I thought only very old cars did this! The only time that I went up in a Harvard two-seater to be shown some aerobatics I had the scare of my life. At the top of

Gamecock rugby team - Air Arm Medical Course.
The author is on the left, middle row.

looping the loop when I was upside down I suddenly could not see out of the front window because of a film of green. My pilot was not too upset and soon righted the plane and we landed safely. A mechanic had failed to secure the filler cap on the oil tank.

On one flight I was taken by plane up to a Royal Naval Air Station called Stretton, which happened to be quite near to my home in Disley. Though I was able to get up there it was difficult to get back easily by public transport and I was therefore only able to stay the night with my parents before having to go back by train.

The Gamecock aerodrome had a secondary use as far as I was concerned. It produced the most enormous field mushrooms. They sometimes were almost ten inches across.

I was seeking to buy a motorcycle because during the war I had been a dispatch rider in the Home Guard and had quite a knowledge of many makes. In the local pub on the other side of the airfield I saw a motorcycle lying on its side in the back near a lot of rubbish. I asked about it and was told that someone had come on it but it broke down and he had left it for the landlord to do with it as he wished.

It had the name Federation on its tank. Later I was told that the Wholesale Co operative Society made it. No-one had ever heard of them and it had a J.A.P. side-valve engine. Remarkably it had no lights. Knowing that J.A.P. engines were very good, I said I would have it and I think I gave £10 for it. In the back of the surgery I took it to pieces having pushed it across the airfield. There was nothing major wrong with it and it went well though being a side valve and only 250cc it was not fast. I got over the problem of no lights by putting a cycle dynamo on to the front wheel and with the help of an Aldis lamp (there were plenty of "spare" lamps in the stores) I was able to provide a circle of light but nothing in the middle. This was the sort of visual field that accompanied a very common eye condition called macular degeneration! So it was fine if one kept moving but no use when stopped. In those days there was little traffic on the roads and the police were not interested. I drove back to Nuneaton many times and had no problems.

The social life was first class and I soon had a number of friends, some engineers, some teachers and of course my dental squash partner. Billiards, snooker and tennis were the main occupations with the odd dance thrown in. Each month there was a mess dinner, which required dressing in mess kit. That was to say short jacket and bow tie. On these occasions one must remember to pass the port to the left or there would be adverse comment.

After doing my small surgery I repaired to the back of the building where I had a room for my repairs on my bike. Otherwise I spent time going round the station, meeting people and reading.

Before Jean had got digs in Nuneaton I had hired a caravan at a little placed called Wolvey about two miles from the station. When I was on call I would be with Jean in this caravan. Since it had no telephone, Sick Berth attendants would come round in a car and tell me of patients. Once I had to look at an X-ray by torchlight to decide if the lad had broken a bone.

Life was easy and sport took up much time. It was usually squash with John Brammer at lunchtime and billiards or snooker in the evening. Tennis, soccer and rugby in summer and winter respectively were the order of the day on either Saturday or Wednesdays. The Sick Berth Chief Petty Officer was the scrum half in the Station rugby team and, of course, he and I got on well together. He was always ribbing me about my lack of knowledge of the Navy. On one occasion when I made some gaffe he put his hand over my watch on my wrist and said, "Tell me Doc, how long have you been in the Navy? Don't look at your watch!"

As the airfield was so close it was ideal for walking when there was no flying. Rabbit shooting too was popular and at weekends the local model airplane club would come and use it for flying their models.

The old Humber despite its proclivity towards always running out

HMS Gamecock Administration Block.

of petrol unexpectedly was still in evidence but it gave so much trouble mechanically that it had to go. At Measham only about 20 miles away the largest car auctions in the country were held. It was there that I said farewell and I got £31 for it, having put a reserve of £30!

One of the slightly unpleasant jobs I had to do was to examine ratings who were in the cells. As one could imagine the usual reason for someone being there at this sort of establishment was for relatively minor offence, usually drunken behaviour and in the worst cases hitting an officer. My job was to confirm the diagnosis of drunkenness as there had been cases of brain damage simulating drunkenness in the later stages.

To keep up my clinical medicine many evenings were spent doing surgeries for a general practitioner in Nuneaton. This was the only time that I did general practice in all my life. It was quite enjoyable though I did not feel it was really for me in the future. I had only one private patient. He ran a shooting gallery in a fairground. I received the princely sum of 7s 6d for each visit! This time was the beginning of the National Health Service but there had been no changes at this stage and clinical examinations were more frequent than hospital investigations.

Occasionally there was a flurry of cleaning and tidying in the Sick Bay at Gamecock when a senior officer – usually an Admiral – came to inspect us. This meant that I tagged on behind the Principal Medical Officer and the VIPs. It was all very perfunctory and I always remember one of these senior officers intoning to himself but heard by me "Death, where is thy sting a ling a ding!" He was as bored with it as we were. Having had a lot of this sort of thing in the Merchant Navy I took it light-heartedly and usually found some humour in it.

After the morning sick parade 'Feddy', my name for my motorbike, was the main focus of interest. His clutch was his weakness and had to be taken to pieces. It was not acceptable for the doctor to have dirty hands so surgical gloves had to be worn at these times.

In those days the waiting list for new cars was long and being quite close to Coventry I had heard that the shortest waiting list was for Singer cars. This was because they were not as popular as Austin, Ford, and Rover etc.. I had had a brochure on the Singer 4AB tourer priced at £585 with a relatively short waiting list. So I put my name down for one, as I was fond of open cars – and still am!

In the meantime my driving was in the GP's almost new Ford Prefect. I did some home visits in this and on one memorable occasion, on Christmas Eve 1951, when the Station was to have its special lunch disaster occurred. I had done the surgery and was in a hurry to get back to Bramcote. The roads were icy and I realised when I put on the brakes that I would slide inexorably into an A40 van at traffic lights! There was nothing I could do but sit there and wait for the crunch. No one was hurt since I was going at about ten miles an hour when we collided. However there was some frontal damage though I could drive on after the usual long statements and exchange of addresses and insurance company details. The sadness was that I was too late for my lunch. The G P was not too upset and the insurance company paid up.

Singer Tourer.

That Christmas was cold and there was a 'flu epidemic. My sick bay was full with ratings with high temperatures. My ward rounds, which used to be almost non-existent, could now take up to an hour.

As had been accentuated, sport was very much to the fore and one of our dentists – John Brammer – had already been noted as the most important opponent. He had a colleague called Jim Bell who unlike John was resident and used to be my snooker and billiard opponent. In those days TV was still very new and only black and white. Most evenings when not playing on the tables we congregated round the 12-inch set. Breakdowns of transmission were not infrequent and the potter with his wheel and the emerging vase was still worthy of our attention.

In the middle of February the great excitement was the arrival of a silver Singer tourer. It had a fold down windscreen and was a full four seater with red upholstery. At this time the quality control on all cars was not very efficient and visits to the factory at Coventry for minor imperfections were quite frequent. It was a lovely looking little car and was considered the poor man's MG. Jean who was having driving lessons was delighted that with the hood down she was able to see exactly where she was and could do reversing and three point turns with great ease. When she eventually took her test she was lucky that the weather was so dry that she was able to have the hood down and she reckons that was the main factor in her passing. Another feature that helped her in her driving test was the knob on the steering wheel. I had brought this back from America where they were quite common and gave an indication of which way the wheels were facing.

Our Queen Alexandra's Nursing Service sister Molly came to the end of her Naval service and was replaced by another sister from Plymouth. Almost at the same time the PMO left too and this time a Surgeon Captain O'Meara took his place. He was much more of a clinician than his predecessor and specialised in atypical pneumonia.

That March I had a fortnight's leave and was able to take Jean in the Singer on a tour of the south coast. We visited Plymouth and went into Dorset and Wiltshire. We did a tour of my old naval haunts but this time with more comfort than in the Humber! The weather was perfect and the car performed well.

In April, bearing in mind that I was scheduled to leave the Navy in July, I started thinking about my future. As I had already said I was not enchanted by the idea of doing general practice, which I knew most of my year, would be doing. My father was what was known in those days as a commercial traveller. Perhaps salesman would be a modern equivalent. He represented works in the Midlands that made specialised metals and because he used to take me to the works where high quality steel parts (for Rolls Royce engines) were forged I got to know something of working conditions. The foundries particularly with heat and dust and danger made me realise that there was a future in looking after the health of such workers. Occupational medicine was just emerging then as a speciality and through the British Medical Journal I sent out applications to Esso Petroleum Company and the National Coal Board. As a result of the former I was short listed for a job as medical officer for the new refinery that was being built in Fawley in Hampshire. The interview in London was with the chief medical officer a Dr Capel. He said something to me that, if I had had a day's notice, would not have floored me as it did. He said, "Sell yourself, Chivers! " I came second.

The National Coal Board had an opening in Doncaster but I did not get an interview.

Since Nuneaton was so near to Birmingham and knowing that the Austin Motor Company employed doctors I made an appointment to see the consultant Dr Donald Stewart and the chief medical officer Dr A A White (I never knew what the A A stood for!) This interview at the end of April was successful. By good fortune the present medical officer, a woman, was pregnant and furthermore had a rather severe neck condition, which made it unlikely she would work again after the baby was born. So I was offered the job with a salary of £800 going up to £1000 a year. I was required to start immediately. The naval authorities were not in a hurry and it was July 16th before I officially left the Royal Navy.

So ended my National Service which started in January 1947 and

HMS Indomitable.

ended in July 1951 – twice as long as any of my contemporaries.

However there was a postscript. Since I had joined the Royal Naval Volunteer Reserve I was obliged to do two weeks' service the following year. I had not been on a ship in the Royal Navy and this promised to put the matter right.

On June 2nd 1952, I went by train to Weymouth, via Bristol and Westbury. The one to Westbury went through beautiful country. The pretty clean stations on the way did not mar the journey through wooded rolling countryside with glimpses of the Avon and boats. Bath, too looked better than when I last saw it from a train and except for my incipient tiredness I would have paid more attention to the surroundings to see if I could recognise any landmarks.

At Westbury there was only a short wait and an almost empty carriage. For the first time I felt that I could talk. Firstly I was at the end of my capacity for reading and secondly the lone man opposite me looked the sort who would talk. The other occupant was a soldier doing his T A training. The man told me he came from Dudley and now worked at Yeovil for the Westland Aircraft Company. He was in charge of the apprentices and told me of his difficulties, rather like my Bramcote friend who went into industry in a similar job. When he left the carriage a woman with a four-month-old baby came in and made me a little anticipatory! (Our first-born's keel had just been laid!) She left and a noble lady with a grudge, which she had to let loose on to us came in. Her grouse was directed towards the bus services which were not as advertised. She was not the sort I wanted to listen to and discreetly closed my eyes! Castle Carey of happy holiday memory was noted but none of its beauty could be seen from the train. So to Weymouth and the first sight of the sea.

I knew there would be a 'bus to Portland but even if the taxi man had not told me there was a long walk to the dockyard I would still had taken it. There was no sign of the Weymouth Jean and I knew until we passed the little inlet where the pleasure boats were. From then on I remembered the drive to Portland Bill. What a difference in the harbour though. The Vanguard (now the flagship), Indefatigable, Indomitable and at least three destroyers and one other battleship were at anchor there. I tried to take a photo but the ships were too far away. A captive balloon, which I was later told was used for radar work flew over the dockyard. The guard at the gates directed the driver to one pier and after I had paid him 10/- (50p) for the five-mile journey he left me.

There ended my shore journey and I was not unhappy to see my destination, though I could not tell which of the three carriers was the Indomitable – the one that I was to go on. I walked to the end of the pier and saw a pinnace with Indomitable in big letters on the side of her cabin. The coxswain told me that they had come to pick up the Captain (Wood, by name) and his wife to take them back to the ship. When the Captain turned up a few minutes later he was in Mess Dress (the garb to be worn at formal dinners) and she was in evening dress.

I had put my cap on so that I could raise it (!) and ask permission to have a lift. This was agreed and he ushered me on first. Later I learned that the Captain was always last on and first off so that he had not to wait. Knowing nothing of the Naval routine I tried to keep my composure whilst making small talk with them both in the cabin. Because of this I had no idea which way we went or which ship of the three was the Indomitable. However when we were alongside a ship up he climbed followed by his wife and then belatedly came Muggins, expecting trouble. Apparently it was correct to go up the Captain's ladder if he had invited you. I could always remember my good friend Bob Broughton who was then a regular doctor in the Navy, saying to me that he had gone first once in Malta causing consternation and a "shower of coals on his head!".

The Lt. Commander addressed me as "Sir" when I stepped on the quarterdeck, which surprised me, but I tried not to show it. Perhaps the presence of the Captain had something to do with this! It was not long before a rating came along and shepherded me to the Mess Office where I was given a Mess Number and a cabin number. Another Surg. Lt. RNVR who had joined the day before for his fortnight's training took me by the arm and whilst we walked towards my cabin he explained one or two things. Firstly, Sunday night (which this was) was a Ladies Night and I had better put on my best uniform and bow tie.

Secondly he said, "You are going to have a wonderful time!" He was a pathologist at the Middlesex Hospital aged about 35. This seemed encouraging. It was difficult to get an idea of what it was like to walk in this vast ship. Bearing in mind that above was a massive deck the length of the corridors and the multiplicity of openings made getting about difficult. I walked along the lower deck forward on the port side (left looking towards the bow) for about two hundred yards in a straight line. After every third yard one had to climb over a coaming of about 18 inches, which was to save seas from washing into the cabins.

After a short way one would come out into the open and then went back into the inner deck. It was all very confusing and as I was talking I did not make a note of all the turns. Everywhere was painted grey and looked well cared for. I was shown the Mess Office and the Wardroom and its galley. Fortunately the Sick Bay was quite close to the wardroom. Since there were 100 officers there was a problem with accommodation. "Our" cabin was an internal one and so had no porthole and the ventilation came through a ducting, which made a swooshing sound. It was much noisier than on the Arawa.

I said "our" cabin because I shared it with a Lt. (P) Ted Scoley (P ... for Pilot) who though a pilot was one of the three "batmen" who guide the 'planes in when they land.

When I arrived he was changing and immediately apologised for the mess the cabin was in. The two bunks were along the two longer walls. There was little room between the bunks and little above and below since this was where there were drawers. A wardrobe and washbasin took up the rest of the space. Due to being an interior cabin it was dark if the light was not switched on. Ted seemed a pleasant enough type who like most pilots I had met, was keen on his beer. I changed and went down with him to the wardroom.

The bar was reputed to be the longest in the Navy and it certainly looked very smart. Many officers were there. I met the two National Service doctors who had been on the ship since last November. One of them had his fiancée on board and both seemed very matey. Christian names were soon used and the atmosphere was congenial. Then to supper where there was a range of cold meats that took some beating. There were nine of them and, of course, I had to hold back a bit! The dining room was just as opulent as the lounge and about twice as big as that at Gamecock. Coffee afterwards in the lounge (or was it anteroom, I'm not sure). Then someone said that there was a film show at 9pm and after I had spoken to Surg. Captain Rudd (MO in charge of Portland Hospital) we went down into the lower hangar to watch a film. "Encore" was the name of the film and how I enjoyed it.

At 11pm I walked in the direction of my cabin part of the way with the RNVR doc who had had an extra day on the ship and knew how to get around. Relying on my memory of the opposite journey a few hours before I kept on alone. When I got to the corridor where my cabin should be I could only see clusters of hammocks. Climbing up and down perpendicular ladders and over coamings occupied another quarter of an hour until I bumped into a Lt. Cmdr. who took me in tow and found my cabin for me. Very kindly he showed me where the lavatories (called in Naval language "heads") were but as this meant at least four cross road turns I had to ask him to take me back or I would have been lost again!

So to bed - Ted was still with the boys. My bunk was alongside the alley way on two sides and the open space where the Midshipmen lived (it was their hammocks which upset my orientation before). On top of my cabin was the crews' mess deck where the budding Fred Astaires kept attempting to break in their new steel toed boots. These horrors might sound exaggerated and indeed all noise was in a strange bed, particularly when one slept between blankets, as I did for that night. Since then I had acquired sheets and pillowcases from the sickbay.

The night passed and at 7am a steward brought me some horrible tea with condensed milk in it. Breakfast made me feel a bit more awake. The sickbay was the next target and with Basil Morson (the other 2 weeker) we saw it in action. To my mind it was badly designed and though there was accommodation for about a dozen bed cases the place looked chaotic. First of all it was close to where the ratings slept and ate, and therefore was noisy and secondly there was one consulting room only approachable via the ward. The bathroom was in the dispensary. The office was used as one consulting room and office work was done in the ward. There were no orderly queues as at Gamecock.

The PMO took me to meet the Captain – formally this time and then we went to the Pay Office and the Captain's Secretary to complete the joining routine. Thanks to walking a lot with others I could make my way from the Wardroom to my cabin with out fear of getting lost though later in the morning when I was taken round the ship by one of the Sick Berth Attendants (SBAs). I realised that I must not venture far off the beaten track. He took us to the top of the island (where the bridge, etc was) and on to the flight deck. Then in order the decks below were the Upper gallery, Upper hangar (where my cabin was), Lower gallery (where the Wardroom and Sick Bay were), main and lower hangar and after that we did not investigate.

Someone had said that I was to help crew a sailing boat that was to be involved in a race. We went back for my raincoat and on returning I saw that there was a 30-foot boat fastened to the end of a boom with someone in it. The boom was a long (about 40 feet) trunk of wood sticking out at right angles to the side of the ship. Normally this boom would lie alongside the ship when at sea but was used for tethering boats whilst in port. I had always thought that they were for the use of ratings but I overestimated the ratings.

The top of the trunk was flat (little comfort when 30 feet off the sea!) and there was a rope running from the ship to the end of the trunk at about the 3 foot level. From this you could gather that we were to get into the boat by this means. I had hopes that the cutter (as the boat was called) would be brought alongside the gangway but as one by one the crew (in warm sweaters and no macs) walked along the plank I knew there was no way out. We had seen from the day's papers that there were gales round the South coast. Sir, I beg to confirm! Whilst I was always ready for a new experience I did not relish the prospect of a very cold bathe and this looked the most certain way of getting it.

The first part of the journey was from the side of the ship over a short grill whilst holding on to a rail until reaching the boom. Walking along that was not difficult except that my mac kept beating against my knocking knees! The rope ladder was not so easy as the wind and the looseness of it made my mac even more of a handicap. Willing hands helped me in and I sank into the stern seat determined to rest until my pulse came down into double figures! This was not to be as all hands were required to raise the mast and get all ready for setting the sails. At 2.15 we were ready and so was the wind. Many yachting terms were used and some unladylike phrases were heard particularly when the sail was half up and flapping fit to burst.

Landing on the flight deck.

Up it went at long last and then the sun shone. I put my coat safely away, as it was delightfully warm. This lasted about two minutes during which time I relaxed at the stern. As I was near the chap holding on to the main sail by a rope I soon had to help him. When the Major, who was at the tiller said "Check the mains" we let the rope out until he said "Abaft the mains" at which we pulled the rope until he said "Well". After a time there were mutterings from my fingers that sounded like the cracking of crabs claws! Worse was to come because, though the cutter keeled over quite alarmingly she always responded to "Checking the mains "whatever that meant! She was required to change direction every few minutes - a manoeuvre called "tacking" and required Muggins (that's me) and my partner also holding the rope "Abafting" for all we were worth ducking under the boom as it crossed over from one side of the boat to the other. We then had to "check" and make sure that the rope was tightened to make the sail fill correctly. This procedure was repeated frequently. A similar though less strenuous procedure was performed for the smaller fore sail.

All this was because I had volunteered to crew in a race for the "Black Cup". This was between the three aircraft carriers and the Vanguard (a large battleship) How it was judged I did not discover but I gathered that it was over a two lap course round the ships in the harbour. At 2.30 p m it started and all was tense from then on. The Surg. Cmdr. and Basil were in the crew. The former was well occupied in baling out water in the bottom of the boat. She heeled over very well and as a result of sliding across the boat on two occasions I took off the slipping half-wellingtons and managed bare-footed.

You could imagine the excitement because of the congestion of big ships and little sailing boats cutting across each other's tracks. I think we were disqualified when the forward look out warned the Major at the tiller of someone on our starboard beam and though action was taken the other boat hit us at full speed just across from where I was sitting. It was an ugly sound the splintering of wood but I was spared the even uglier sound of gurgling water entering, due to the cutter's stout bulwarks. Recriminations did no good and after we had checked or "abafted" we went on.

So for two hours we sailed round the ships and the only other real excitement was a Portuguese destroyer which was trying to get alongside another ship of its own nationality. Because of the weather and their poor seamanship they kept taking runs at the buoy but kept failing. On two of these runs we had to get out of her way as "she was bigger than us" She was always referred to as the "Portugoose!" or the

"Goose" Slightly salted we returned to Indomitable and came alongside the gangway. No one got off. The mast was lowered, everything stowed away and the cutter was pulled to - the boom! This time I had sent my coat via a bucket to the ship and managed the rope ladder with out much trouble. At the top I could not get my foot on to anything to lift myself on to the boom. It was an odd experience balancing with half on one side and half on the other. I had to push myself over the head side to get my feet on to the flat of the boom. After that I was able to stand. The reason for my trouble was my choice of the motor boat ladder, which was reputed to be more difficult. My legs were like jellies as I walked along the boom back to the ship. I had still to hear how we did in the race but I treasured it as a unique experience.

After an early supper I went to bed. On waking we were at sea and had been for a few hours. The daily papers had come on board however. Until 10.30 Basil and I watched one plane take off by catapult and one without any run. The latter was a helicopter, which an R A F pilot brought on board. At 10.30 we were asked to help to do PULHEEMS. This took me back to the Royal Arthur days. The four of us took different systems - I did muscles in the morning and heart and lungs in the afternoon. In about three hours we saw 70 odd candidates (I must not call them "patients") It was deadly boring and I hated it but these two RNVR docs had over 800 to do on the ship besides over 900 inoculations. The Pulheems and injections should have been done in the Barracks as there was quite a lot of other work to be done here.

That afternoon I watched Hornets (2 engined night fighters) land after doing the second lot of Pulheems. There was a flying doctor on board. He was a Lt Cmdr with the 820 squadron. His job was research at Farnborough and he was supposed to be batman on this cruise though he had been flying to day.

Indomitable was built in 1940 but had been in reserve for some time prior to coming into service again 3 years ago. Her maximum speed was 30 knots though she only did 24 that day. Vampires (jets) should have landed in the afternoon but because of the lack of wind (and this meaning maximum speed from the ship was required) they did not come. Ted told me that the batsman liked a total of about 30 knots of wind, 15 natural and 15 made by the ship. The ship was 750 feet long and 57 feet wide and weighed 26,000 tons. It had a complement of 1,500 men including about a hundred officers. There were four engines (oil –fired steam turbines) driving four propellers. The engines developed 11,000-horse power. The Eagle, which was another carrier, had a width of 120 feet – a bit of useless information!

After dinner I was taken to see the long hangar where the squadron's planes were. I was shown the inside of the Firefly twin seater that this pilot friend of mine looked after. These were used for anti-submarine work and had an observer. The system of catching wires, that stopped the planes on landing, lay under the main flight deck and could be seen in this hangar. There must have been a terrific noise when these were pulled. The wires were at the stern end of the ship and the batman tried to make the plane catch the fourth wire with its tail hook. The wires pulled on hydraulic rams and if the plane missed them she hit the wire net barriers which usually upended the plane. This was a very rare occurrence. I was also shown the lifts, which took up to 6 tons of plane with bombs.

By this time we were anchored in Torbay and we could see the carrier "Triumph" there. It was a lovely view at night time. The following day we were at sea. In the morning we towed a target for the Fireflies to fire rockets at. In return the ship shot targets pulled by planes with the 4.5 anti-aircraft guns. They certainly shook the ship and all in her. Though I watched some landings later in the morning most of the time in the last two days had been spent doing Pulheems. The four of us still took systems and my ears were sore because I was back on "chests" – the stethoscope's friction was beginning to be painful. This wretched procedure lasted two minutes and the whole session about two hours.

I felt that due to the conditions the work here was unhealthy. Only those on the flight deck could get reasonable light and air. Rarely did one see the sun once down inside the hull. When flying was in progress one could not sit about on a deck partly because there was no deck space but also because of the noise and activity. After a couple of hours in the Sick Bay I longed for my open car and a run in the countryside.

After that short spell at sea we were back again at Torbay. That night there was night flying with the Hornets from the air base at Culdrose. They came to practise deck landing until 1am. Although it was moonlight one could see little of the aircraft except their landing lights. Because of their width, speed and the dark the effect could be well imagined. The impression was always that they were right on top of one and would crash into the bridge. The speed of the ship was about 25 knots to give them 35 knots across the deck. This caused some shudder but it was not until I got to bed at midnight that the shudder became worse.

Speed was increased and the effect was like lying in a car without

HMS Apollo.

tyres or springs whilst driving over cobbles! This only lasted for half an hour and then I went to sleep.

It was the Queen's birthday the following day and to commemorate it there was a fly past of all the planes on the ship. All officers and ratings were lined up on the flight deck. The ship was dressed with flags and 21 rounds of 4.5 ammunition were fired. Then like a comic act - the after lift which was at the lower hangar level was raised with the Captain and the Admiral (Casper John – Admiral commanding the Heavy squadron) on it. There was no inspection and only a gramophone record of "God Save the Queen". We all went down and had a drink with the Admiral.

He was the son of Augustus John the famous painter and some said that Augustus was proud of him as he was the only successful son he was sure was legitimate! I was taken to meet the Paymaster of the Apollo (a minelayer). I had had a conversation with a Surg. Cmdr. who had asked me whether I would like to go for the second week on the Apollo. The Paymaster said that there was no problem. Captains of both Apollo and Indomitable also had no objections so it was arranged I went the following day.

That afternoon I went ashore to watch tennis in Torquay. This was held at the Torquay Tennis Club and since it was a championship I was able to see Drobny (a Wimbledon finalist) play in the quarterfinals, which he won. It was surprisingly enjoyable to get into fresh air and not be surrounded by men in uniforms. To cap it all we had a delicious Devon tea complete with cream and strawberry jam on the scones.

One of the small compensations for the conditions on an aircraft carrier was the varied papers and periodicals that were flown in each day. They included Esquire, Life, New Yorker and the Saturday Evening Post

My departure from Indomitable like my arrival was in the Captain's barge but this time it was for me alone. The time was 9.15 am and when I arrived on Apollo there were only two of the normal dozen officers on board. As it was a Plymouth ship the rest who were not on duty had gone to Plymouth "just for the ride" as the Senior Engineer delicately put it.

My impressions of this ship were not so complicated by the difficult geography, which I had met in Indomitable. She was a mine-layer built in 1941, but was in reserve for some years. Her tonnage was 4,000 odd unloaded without her 150 mines.

Her appearance was similar to a destroyer without the cutaway aft portion. This was the mine deck and to get to the wardroom one had to pass through it. If you had been in a cross channel train ferry the sight would be familiar. Lanes ran up and down both sides of the deck to the stern where they came together at doors, which opened to the sea. Rows of mines (without horns and marked "dummy") sat on the rails.

The wardroom was dining room and ante-room combined and had loose covers on the upholstery that made it cheerful and cosy. It was very inviting after the expanse of the Indomitable. I had a drink with the officer of the watch ('Sub' he was called) and Sec (Captain's secretary who was also my cabin mate). These two were the only bachelors on board. Sec was very new in the Service and bought books that dubbed him a bachelor before he told me. Later the Commander (E) – engineer – came on board in civvies and in his cups!

He talked nonsense to me for about an hour but remembered none of it the following morning. Most of the officers were Lt Cmdrs. A 'Torpedo Anti-Submarine officer was in charge of the mine-laying. There was a First Lieutenant, a Pilot (navigator), Senior Engineer and a Gunnery Officer, all of whom were Lieutenant Commanders. That was the way the Navy afloat had become because of the shortage of ships.

My cabin was a little better than on the Indomitable though it was still internal. It had slightly more space. I was on the top bunk and slept quite well until 7.30am.

At breakfast (bangers!) I met some of the officers already mentioned. A little later I was taken up on to the bridge to watch us arrive back into Portland harbour. Each time we passed another R N ship we dipped our Ensign and we all saluted. It was difficult to decide which way to face since there were so many!

The Sick Berth Petty Officer had been a male nurse in BOAC until he was called up to do his 18 months with the Royal Fleet Reserve. There he had been the 'Doc' but seemed a pleasant type. The Sick Bay had only two berths but there was no need for anything bigger as there were only 230 men on board. He asked if I had a diagnostic set, as there were 30 PULHEEMS to do! I told him I had not and hoped he would not be able to acquire one before I left the ship. I had hoped to escape PULHEEMS after the Indomitable sausage machine.

The ship had a couple of engines similar in type to the Indomitable but developing 76,000-horse power. When designed she was intended to do 39 knots. The papers called it 40 and later more than 40. In actual fact she could do about 35 which was still the fastest in the Navy (except for small launches which could do up to 45) The reason for this was to get in and out of trouble as quickly as possible. Laying the mines took under 20 minutes (1 mine every 6 seconds) the speed was kept below 20 knots for this part of the operation. Knots may be converted into miles per hour by adding 1/8th – thus our maximum speed was almost 40 miles per hour.

We were to stay at Portland for a few days because we were to have an inspection by C-in-C Portland. The following day, Sunday, we would go to Portsmouth and then on to Rosyth to pick up dummy mines and to have speed trials.

After all that Apollo would take part in "Castenets" – some sort of exercise. An interesting job was watched in the afternoon when a diver mended a hole in the side of the ship. This hole was some sort of induction feed for the engine room and the engineers wanted to do some repairs to a gland in the pipe. As it was only a matter of going down 29 feet the diver used a light rubber suit and headgear and carried his own oxygen.

Shortly after this there was a practice mine-laying exercise and I went to the stern on the mining deck to see it. The mines were tethered to the deck above so that they could be hauled on board afterward and, of course, were all dummies. The long 'railway lines' tracks lead to the opening at the stern – normally closed by sliding watertight doors. One of these lines had a set of points so that there could be a continuous flow of mines since they were all linked together. Each mine was lashed to a box like structure or cradle and alongside it a circular weight.

The operation was that they all went out like a string of sausages and when they hit the water the wooden structure and the heavy weight separated though they were both still attached to the mine. The weight went to the bottom of the sea and the wooden structure and the mine were suspended so that the mine was at a critical depth in order to be hit by a ship usually about ten feet below.

The heavyweight when it touched the seabed pulled on a mechanism in the mine that actuated it. This rather complicated action was very swift. The Captain watched with me, as he had not seen it before himself. All went well until the last of the four test mines broke loose and its base disappeared and the mine came to the surface. A diver was brought out to get the base. As it was down 60 feet a deep-sea diver was required which meant there was to be more excitement yet! It was recovered the following day after much work.

The following morning was a disappointment because a Commodore of the Swedish Navy and an Engineer Admiral had been on board and I could not go down to the engine room as I had intended, as this was where they were going to do the inspection. As we were at anchor I had attempted to fish, after considerable trouble with making a line. The Captain who was showing the Swedish Commodore round saw me. The former told me that I was breaking 'every law in the Navy!' and told me to get the line up at once. Apparently one should not fish during working hours.

I managed to get ashore at Weymouth and was pleased to see Portuguese and Norwegian matelots mingling with our sailors. Back on board I had a conversation with the Captain who became quite friendly when I promised I would do the 30 Pulheems that were outstanding! When he had joined this ship he had just got his fourth ring on his sleeve. Previously he had had the reputation of being the rudest Commander in the Navy!

Apollo had not been well preserved whilst it had been in reserve and since getting her out a year ago there had been a lot of work to do on her. I heard that Apollo had been the relief ship to Kingston when they had had their hurricane. This morning the C in C Portland came out from Vanguard and inspected us at Divisions. Divisions were held each day with the men in-groups all round the main deck.

My cap did not look so smart and lack of medals, sword and gloves made me feel that perhaps I would be better out of the way. Apollo's Captain had said I was to be there so there I was! The Admiral spoke to me and asked what I did and as head of the department I had to follow the Admiral, Captain, Engineer Cmdr. and Paymaster. There was nothing to it and all went well. Prayers and a hymn on this Quarter-

The mine discharge port.

A mine on deck.

deck (stern) afterwards was pleasant enough and the all-male chorus seemed well in tune.

When we left Portland the Senior Engineer took me down to the engine room as she got under way. Surprisingly enough it was quite cool where he controlled the engines but there were other parts, which were hot. There was much less room than in the Merchant Navy ships but this was to be expected.

We anchored near the Birmingham, a cruiser, and the reserve carrier 'Formidable'. We were off Spithead and it took half an hour to get ashore. Because of this and the fact that it was a wet evening I stayed on the ship and watched a film.

The following day was spent in taking off all the mines and ammunition prior to filling up with more at Rosyth. Fishing was no good here as the current was too fast. This I found out in the afternoon but it was pleasant to look around and gaze at ships passing. The liner America and two submarines came by besides numerous small craft. Facing us was Haslar (where the naval hospital was) and Southsea, of happy memories.

A Lieutenant Wardle came for drinks in the evening. He was from HMS Vernon - the HQ of the naval diving school where he was chief instructor. He had been in charge of the attempts to get into a sunken submarine called "Affray". He felt that putting down TV cameras was a waste of time and that time could have been more used in getting divers in. Because of the danger of 'oxygen poisoning' at great depths helium was mixed with it. The danger was still present however of "bends" and a decompression chamber was lowered to around 160 feet for a first stage where the diver could be adjusted.

The next morning we were up the Firth of Forth and under the famous bridge on our way to Rosyth. My time was spent doing PULHEEMS as an auriscope had been obtained from the depot. I projected my thoughts to the power trials, which we would be having in a day or so. In the meantime the ship was being loaded with 100 dummy mines. Despite the possibility of the 40 knots the speed trials did not reach anything like that figure, as the senior engineer was frightened of blowing up the engines!

Having fulfilled my promise to the Captain and done the PULHEEMS I got myself ready to say farewell to this exciting ship and return to civvy life and a severing of my last link with my bizarre National Service.

As a Post Script to what would appear to have been a waste of two years' clinical time it is worth recording that these experiences have helped me a great deal in life. I feel that not only had travel given me self-confidence and more knowledge of the world, but also introduced me to a range of people who helped my understanding of human nature.

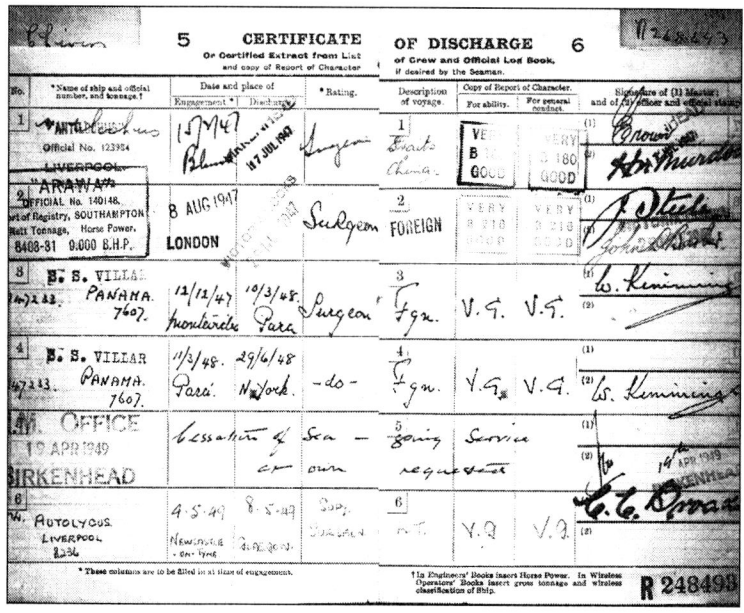

Author's "Continuous Certificate of Discharge".

APPENDIX

The cargo on the Antilochus when she left Birkenhead bound for the Far East:
Ink, distemper, knives, battery tools, motor cars, gauze and lint, machinery, cycle parts, kegs of paint, radios, asbestos sheets, electric fittings, bags of sulphur, bales of blanket, twist drills, piston rings, cigarette papers, surgical sundries, cases of medicines, crockery, oil cloth, tyres, tubes, garage equipment, electric kettles, coils of copper wire. Wire netting, cinema equipment, talcum powder, drums of paint and sulphuric acid and zinc chloride and other chemicals, cylinders of carbonic acid, cases of hoe heads, gramophone needles, golf clubs, footballs, dyes, cases of cigarettes, cases of toilet preparations, kennel and dogs, drums of oil, brilliantine, aluminium ware, fish hooks, disinfectant, shot guns, chocolate, electric cookers, cisterns, confectionery, cycles, buckets, artificial silks, textiles (a large quantity) stout, whisky, sugar, formic acid (for the rubber plantations), dredge buckets, (to Port Swettenham to clean out the muck in the creeks), biscuits, Dragon's blood, sharks fins, dried prawns.

Far East to Liverpool:
Sundries, copra, sago flour, rubber, coconut oil, palm oil, peanuts, hemp, hides, jam, palm kernels, latex, lead, seed tapioca, pear tapioca, pepper, rattans, pearl sago, rifles, wolfram, carboys.

Aden to Liverpool:
Cars, lighthouse equipment, cigarettes and calf skins.